Quality and Competence

The Kogan Page Practical Trainer Series

Series Editor: Roger Buckley

Competence-Based Assessment Techniques Shirley Fletcher
Cost-Effective Training Tony Newby
Designing Competence-Based Training Shirley Fletcher
How to Design and Deliver Equal Opportunities Training Judith Taylor and Helen Garrett
How to Design and Deliver Induction Training Programmes Michael Meighan
How to Design and Deliver Quality Service Training Tony Newby
How to Design and Deliver Retirement Training Marcella Bailey and Peter Reynolds
How to Design and Introduce Appraisal Training Carol McCallum
How to Take a Training Audit Michael Applegarth
How to Write and Prepare Training Materials Nancy Stimson
The In-House Trainer as Consultant Mike Saunders and Keith Holdaway
The Lone Trainer Mike Saunders and Keith Holdaway
Managing Training Sunny Stout
One-to-One Training and Coaching Skills Roger Buckley and Jim Caple
A Practical Approach to Group Training David Leigh
Selecting and Using Training Aids David Flegg and Josephine McHale
Training for Total Quality Management David R Jeffries, Bill Evans and Peter Reynolds
Training Needs Analysis in the Workplace Robyn Peterson
Validating Your Training Tony Newby

PRACTICAL TRAINER SERIES

KOGAN PAGE

Quality and Competence

Integrating Competence and Quality Initiatives

SHIRLEY FLETCHER

KOGAN PAGE
Published in association with the
Institute of Training and Development

First published in 1993

Apart from any fair dealing for the purposes of research or private study, or criticism or review, as permitted under the Copyright, Designs and Patents Act, 1988, this publication may only be reproduced, stored or transmitted, in any form or by any means, with the prior permission in writing of the publishers, or in the case of reprographic reproduction in accordance with the terms of licences issued by the Copyright Licensing Agency. Enquiries concerning reproduction outside those terms should be sent to the publishers at the undermentioned address:

Kogan Page Limited
120 Pentonville Road
London N1 9JN

© Shirley Fletcher, 1993

British Library Cataloguing in Publication Data

A CIP record of this book is available from the British Library.

ISBN 0 7494 0706 9

Typeset by Koinonia Ltd, Bury
Printed and bound in Great Britain by
Biddles Ltd, Guildford and King's Lynn

Contents

Series Editor's Foreword *Roger Buckley*   8

Preface   10

Acknowledgements   11

Introduction   13
    Do You Need to Read This Book?   13
    What Prompted Me to Write It?   14
    Using This Book   15
    Chapter Summaries   16

1 Concepts and Objectives   18
    The Quality and Competence Divide   18
    What Do We Mean by Quality?   18
    Quality Assurance   19
    Competence   19
    What Do We Mean by Integration?   20
    Why Integrate Quality and Competence?   21
    The Driving Force for Change   22
    An Integrative Approach   22
    Case Study   23

2 How Might an Integrative Model Work?   33
    Competence and BS5750/ISO9000   33
    Integrating Competence and Quality Procedures   36
    Competence and TQM   37
    The Issue of Overlap   38
    Developing an Integrative System   38

3 **The Starting Point**   42
   Quality and Competence Are Not
      Mutually Exclusive   42
   Planning and Action   43
   Dialogue and Integration   44
   Initiative Overload Syndrome   46
   Identifying the Starting Point   47
   Taking the First Step   49

4 **The Framework for Integration – Researching and Reporting** **54**
   Preparing the Ground   55
   The Quality Strategy   56
   The Strategic Orchestra   57
   Creating Harmony   60

5 **The Integration Framework**   **63**
   The Strategic Management Group   64
   The Strategic Integration Group   68
   Establish Central Management   74
   The Next Steps   76
   Case Study - Network SouthEast   77

6 **The Operational Plan**   **84**
   Overview   85
   Starting at the Top   85
   Unpacking the Key Purpose of the Company   86
   Developing Competences   90
   The Need for a Common Language   93
   Creating the Common Language   95

7 **Implementing the System**   **99**
   Development Phase   100
   Getting Help   100
   Implementation Phase   100
   Competence and Assessment   103
   Competence and Quality Managers   105
   Competence and Time Management   106
   Competence and Quality Training   107
   Competence and Quality Selection and Recruitment   108
   Competence and Performance Appraisal   109
   Competence and Quality Incentive Systems   109
   Commitment to Change   110

8 National and Organizational Perspectives   **112**
Nationally Derived Competence-based Systems   113
Company-specific Systems   114

References and Further Reading   116

Index   **117**

Series Editor's Foreword

Organizations get things done when people do their jobs effectively. To make this happen they need to be well trained. A number of people are likely to be involved in this training by identifying the needs of the organization and of the individual, by selecting or designing appropriate training to meet these needs, by delivering it and assessing how effective it was. It is not only 'professional' or full-time trainers who are involved in this process; personnel managers, line managers, supervisors and job holders are all likely to have a part to play.

This series has been written for all those who get involved with training in some way or another, whether they are senior personnel managers trying to link the goals of the organization with training needs or job holders who have been given responsibility for training newcomers. Therefore, the series is essentially a practical one which focuses on specific aspects of the training function. This is not to say that the theoretical underpinnings of the practical aspects of training are unimportant. Anyone seriously interested in training is strongly encouraged to look beyond 'what to do' and 'how to do it' and to delve into the areas of why things are done in a particular way. The series has become so popular that it is intended to include additional volumes whenever a need is found for practical guidelines in some area of training.

The authors have been selected because they have considerable practical experience. All have shared, at some time, the same difficulties, frustrations and satisfactions of being involved in training and are now in a position to share with others some helpful and practical guidelines.

In this book, Shirley Fletcher focuses on a potential problem area for many trainers. The many 'quality' initiatives that are being introduced, particularly by large organizations, can leave the trainer, if not the whole workforce, in something of a quandary. The problem is that often there is little or no co-ordination of initiatives introduced by different departments. In linking quality with competence, this book provides a model which shows how all parties can be brought together, with senior management, to establish policy and priority in working towards a common end.

ROGER BUCKLEY

Preface

Many companies, and the managers, decision makers and trainers within them, find themselves halfway through the development of quality projects such as BS5750 and TQM, only to be met by yet another 'quality concept' – competence.

The situation becomes even more difficult when one realizes that similarities between these various initiatives can, and do, create an enormous amount of duplication of effort and increase complexity to unmanageable proportions.

There is, therefore, a need to integrate, to build on what is, after all, a common thread in these developments. *The pursuit of quality assurance in products and services requires a competent workforce, with each individual operating at clearly specified standards of performance. A system of competence-based standards requires a quality assurance mechanism to maintain consistency of performance.*

This book draws on experience with a range of blue chip clients from around the world and outlines a model for integration which builds on a common thread. This model has been developed by Godfrey Durham International Holdings, and copyright materials from this model, known as IBIS (Individual and Business Improvement Strategy), have been included.

The book provides guidance for decision makers, managers and trainers.

Acknowledgements

The author would like to acknowledge the contributions and support of the many clients who have provided feedback and review of the work undertaken with them, as well as the effort made by those who attempted to prepare case studies but were unable to do so within the publishing deadline.

In particular, I would like to thank Doug Hunter, Training and Development Manager, Network SouthEast, for putting in extra time to complete a case study; and Della, for her wizardry in producing illustrations.

Introduction

Do You Need to Read This Book?

Quality and Competence has been written to help you, as manager, trainer or personnel specialist, to integrate and improve your company projects and initiatives.

Many of you will be involved in or managing some aspect of at least one 'quality' initiative. It may be Total Quality Management, or BS5750 quality procedures, or the international ISO9000. It could be a customer service programme, or a 'new ways of working' project or you may be struggling with the introduction of a new 'competence-based' system.

It is more likely that you are involved in several of these initiatives – each demanding your time and that of your staff.

The development and introduction of many competence-based and quality-focused initiatives require similar, if not identical activities by working groups. To expect groups and individuals to attend several briefings, workshops and meetings to review the same data in a different way simply creates frustration and thus dooms any project to failure.

This is an increasingly common phenomenon in companies around the world. Phrases such as 'competing for management time' can be heard ringing, not simply through the corridors of multinational corporations, but across the open-plan spaces of small- to medium-sized organizations.

All of these projects and initiatives are (or should be) aimed at improving business performance, and your role within these projects is crucial to their success. Yet the fact is that many projects fail, or don't even get off the ground, due to the fact that the people involved don't really understand what the project is about or how it fits in with other projects, or what its real objectives are. You may be confused by the different terminology used in different initiatives. There may be competition between different projects, each having its 'champion', each fighting for funding and support. There is always conflict about time – which 'project briefing' or 'training programme' are you going on today? How is this affecting your normal work load?

If any of these comments prompts you to nod in agreement or recognition then this book will be of help to you.

What Prompted Me to Write It?

During the last decade, I have worked intensively in the field of competence-based developments. This is not an amazingly new trend – it has been around for years – but since the latter 1980s, it has exploited new methods and applications (for once, led by the UK) which have been adopted around the world.

Like many trainers, my early involvement in such systems included the use of various concepts of 'competence', most requiring some kind of 'profiling' or 'competence descriptor'; and in various approaches to Japanese-style 'quality management'. UK policy-makers planned the use of industry-defined competence-based standards as the basis for a new structure of National Vocational Qualifications – an idea which was to be taken up by many other countries.

While the concept behind a competence-based approach is sound, its use only as a basis for a national qualification system failed to utilize its full potential as a tool for business improvement. It is the standards-based system itself which holds the real value for improvement of business performance. Building on my background in training and development, I felt strongly that the integration of a competence-based approach was the real key to business success through people.

Although many companies espouse the total quality route, and have 'mission statements' and 'quality policies' displayed in and around the offices, few people actually understand them. Even more interestingly, when projects are introduced they are rarely related directly to these major commitments.

When a company is interested in introducing a competence-based system, one of the first things to ask is, 'How do you see this contributing to your strategic planning?' Often, this has not really been considered, perhaps because companies feel an obligation to introduce (another) national 'scheme' and this is the main motivation or 'driving force'.

The issue of 'driving force' is a key to success. If a new system or method of working is introduced simply because 'it is a national obligation' or 'someone championed it' it will probably fail within its first year.

Even when introduction is linked to a specific aspect of business operation such as 'improving training' or 'raising quality of production', it is unlikely to have the expected major impact unless it is also linked to strategic objectives and integrated with other initiatives. The lack of such integration creates duplication of effort, complexity of development and increased costs.

Exploring and solving these issues with a wide variety of clients led to the development of an integrative model which focuses on efficient and cost-effective use of resources in the development of a performance management system. Most importantly, the model provides a common language as an organizational tool, thus bringing together the various strands of competence and quality intiatives to form a coherent, flexible and practical operational framework.

Using This Book

Quality and Competence provides an overview of the integrative model and guidance on how to implement it. It will not make you an expert in all the activities involved; you will still need to draw on specialist expertise either within your own company or from an external source. However, it will provide a framework and route map to ensure that your plans for strategic integration and cost effective improvement are successfully implemented.

I am an advocate of presentations in plain English. I also prefer approaches which are logical and present ideas in their simplest form. I have consistently found that such an approach leads to more effective and faster progress – and better results. I have therefore tried to present this book in line with these beliefs. I have included descriptions of recent work with various clients to illustrate key points and a case study from one organization which has discovered the value of an integrative approach.

The model has six simple steps, but operating the model is an iterative process. It requires the establishment of a dialogue between planning and action (see Chapter 2) and the review and adjustment of actions of change. You will find, therefore, that chapter titles do not relate directly to these six steps, although the book is structured to take you through the model in logical sequence. You will need to work through the text and activities chapter by chapter.

To help you make best use of the text, tasks and diagrams, the following chapter summaries are provided.

Chapter Summaries

In Chapter One the concepts of 'quality' and 'competence' are outlined, together with an overview of the need for integration. The steps in the model are also introduced. First reactions to this outline of the model will no doubt be, 'Oh, but it's too simplistic!' If this is your reaction, I am delighted. One of the key difficulties experienced by many companies is the complexity of language and approach used. Similarly, there is a mistaken belief that for something to be worth doing, it must be shrouded in complex terminology and 'look impressive' – at the same time being accompanied by cries of 'Why does it have to be so complicated?'

Chapter 2 briefly explores how an integrative system might work and the potential overlap and duplication that exists in the introduction of various initiatives. I suggest that what is needed is a dialogue between planning and action. Figure 2.1 illustrates an operational framework for an integrative model.

Chapter 3 explores 'initiative overload' – you may find some points of identification with other companies' struggles here. This chapter also introduces the *first step* in the model: 'Establish your starting point'. You will find some activities in this chapter to help you with this and to start you off in the preparation of a report and action plan.

Chapter 4 provides guidance on *step two* – 'Clarify objectives'. Action by you in this chapter will include undertaking some research and mapping within your company, reviewing what I have called the 'strategic orchestra'.

You will be able to begin adding meat to the bones of your action plan in Chapter 5, which examines *step three* – 'Establish an integration framework'. This activity requires involvement and commitment of the management team – top-down commitment is essential to the success of any project. This chapter stresses the importance of clear communication based on clarity of objectives. It also includes a case study provided by Network SouthEast.

Chapter 6 focuses on the 'Operational plan' *(step four)* and deals with issues of ownership, involvement and commitment (the OIC approach) in developing a common language for use in all future human resource activities. It also suggests how this common language can be developed, drawing on a synthesis of methodologies and taking the best from each in order to meet business operational needs and to ensure ownership of the standards-based system. This chapter will provide a basis for specification of external support for those who wish to seek such help in the development and/or implementation phases of the model.

Chapter 7 deals with *steps five and six* – 'Develop staff' and 'Implement, monitor and evaluate'. The ripple effect of a competence-based system is introduced, and guidance on getting help with both the development and implementation phases is provided. The potential of a system of competence-based standards is enormous; what I have tried to do is outline a few of the major uses in order to stimulate ideas.

Chapter 8 really stands alone for use as a brief reference or general guide for anyone struggling with decisions regarding national versus company-specific systems. Such decisions need to be informed ones – an outline is therefore provided of some of the key issues and implications involved.

1 Concepts and Objectives

▷   SUMMARY   ◁

This chapter
- explains key concepts used in this book and sets a case for the integration of initiatives.

The Quality and Competence Divide

Throughout the world, national policy-makers and organizations' decision-makers continue to grapple with the problems of achieving quality. Fads and fashions come and go, terminology changes, new initiatives and models emerge.

It appears that the 1990s have introduced yet another quality concept to the leading edge of business improvement activities – competence. In particular, the use of competence-based systems as a foundation of new national qualification frameworks is being adopted by many countries around the world.

Both quality and competence are terms which can be (and are) interpreted in many ways. It is perhaps little wonder then that the introduction of initiatives to improve either or both often fails to achieve its objective.

What Do We Mean by Quality?

The terms 'quality' and 'quality initiative' tend to be used as global terms and one can never be sure exactly which topic of 'quality' is under discussion – and raising the question can often reveal quite disparate answers!

In business terms, 'quality' usually refers to quality of product or services. A quality initiative may be a Japanese-style Total Quality Programme, or a project to establish a manual of quality procedures such as BS5750 or ISO9000.

This book focuses on the issue of quality assurance and the integration of competence-based systems within a quality assurance system.

Quality Assurance

Quality assurance is a process of assuring quality of products and services. In order to operate a quality assurance (QA) system, one must obviously first define the quality one is aiming to achieve – this provides the target or standard by which performance (business, group or individual) can be measured.

The simplest way to envisage this abstract concept of QA is to think of it as a simple and effective management system, thus avoiding a common tendency to overcomplicate any planning and action associated with its introduction.

The focus of quality assurance is to achieve a 'right first time' approach, thus reducing the rate and associated costs of failure through poor products and services. The importance of this 'right first time' approach increases in relation to the organization's cost of failure.

For example, a company which installs deep sea optic fibre cables will incur a high cost of failure if its products and services do not meet specified standards.

This requires that suppliers provide components which meet specifications, and that staff are competent in their work roles. We can identify here, one of the first, and major links between quality and competence.

Competence

The term 'competence' is also open to various interpretations. There are various competence-based systems and concepts of competence.

As a general definition, a competent individual can perform a work role in a wide range of settings over an extended period of time.

This is a broad statement, based on that produced by the UK Department of Employment as the conceptual base of their Standards Development Programme. The UK system focuses particularly on vocational/occupational competence, supplemented by a model of personal competence. Other models focus more on aspects of personal competence, or on the differentiation between competence and excellence.

For our purposes, however, the above definition encompasses both vocational (or occupational) competence and personal competence as requirements for effective operation in a work role. The model detailed in later chapters is very firmly set in the business context and therefore relates to competent performance at work – ie, what we expect people to be able to do in their normal working day.

Competence-based systems are currently being developed and implemented around the world.

Some are development-led: they focus on the development of competence and are therefore linked to training and development programmes – to develop people to a level of performance expected at work.

Others are achievement-led: they focus on assessment of competent performance – what people do at work and how well they do it.

This is an important distinction when considering competence-based systems as the system may include many components, each linking to a different aspect of human resource activity within a business organization. It is essential that, when discussing 'competence' per se, and 'competence-based systems' in general, those involved in the discussion are all talking on the same wavelength!

What Do We Mean by Integration?

Each company may have a number of projects underway or planned, each may be part of an overarching initiative with a grand title such as Change 2000. Links between these projects may be established in general terms, but there is usually a lack of a clear and precise masterplan which outlines in detail how each project operates, what its objectives are and how these objectives *interface* with those of other projects.

'Integration of Quality and Competence' therefore refers to a model by which the planning and implementation of change projects can be brought together to form a coherent route map of organizational development. The model outlined in this book includes the development of a 'common language' as the basis on which all initiatives can develop and operate, thus facilitating the extension of quality improvements to all aspects of business operation with clear communication and confirmation of understanding.

> **DUPLICATION OF EFFORT**
>
> **DUPLICATION OF COST**
>
> **OUTCOMES NOT RELATED TO BUSINESS OBJECTIVES**
>
> **COMPLEXITY OF OPERATION**
>
> **CONFUSED TERMINOLOGY**

Figure 1.1 *Costs of not integrating quality and competence initiatives*

Why Integrate Quality and Competence?

All projects and initiatives should have objectives which contribute to the improvement of business performance. If these projects are undertaken in isolation, the results can not only be confusing, but costly. We therefore need to examine the costs of not integrating, shown in Figure 1.1.

Duplication of Effort and Cost

In financial terms, the duplication of effort involved in operating two or more projects with similar objectives results in increased costs – costs of staff time being of prime importance. Similarly, if external support is required, costs are further duplicated as these external agencies undertake similar activities within the company.

Outcomes Not Related To Business Objectives

If the planning has been ineffective, it is unlikely that any project will achieve objectives that directly contribute to company aims. However, if the planning and action dialogue fails to integrate two or more projects, the failure is doubled, staff motivation is reduced and costs are increased. The return on investment is therefore minimal.

Complexity of Operation

Each project introduces its own terminology and tools. Some may require quality records to be produced, others may require team reports, others require assessment documentation. If projects are introduced in one department and not another, communication may become limited, as understanding and operation of processes and procedures differs.

Confused Terminology

If people are speaking different 'languages' (ie, TQM terminology vs BS5750 terminology vs competence-based assessment terminology) there is little chance of effective communication and even less chance of successful operation in the broad term of achieving business objectives.

The Driving Force for Change

As with all trends, there has been a driving force behind the introduction of both quality initiatives and those relating to competence. These driving forces stimulate action and while the stimulation for action on total quality may be the need to improve product quality, and the stimulation for action on competence may be a need to improve training, both have an overall objective of improving company performance.

Those focused on statistical quality control and its benefits for the manufacturing process will no doubt feel that total quality is about prevention of faults in the production process. Those whose focus is more people-oriented will suggest that total quality is a concept relating to culture, management style and involvement of all employees at all levels.

The interest in competence has been driven by other forces – and currently mainly by government interest in improving the adaptability, mobility and effectiveness of the national workforce. Thus national competence-based systems are being developed and implemented in the UK, Australia, New Zealand, Canada and Denmark (to name but a few). These national systems are usually linked to one of two key aspects of employee development and incentive – training and qualifications.

In the midst of these developments a valuable organizational tool exists – as yet unrecognized. This book aims to increase awareness of that tool by outlining a plan for the integration of these two major trends in business development and illustrating the benefits that such an integrative approach can provide for any organization.

An Integrative Approach

Quality and competence are inextricably linked, and yet so often regarded as totally different, independent approaches to change. To operate an effective quality assurance system a company requires competent people; and to ensure competence of people a company needs a quality assurance mechanism.

ESTABLISH STARTING POINT
(the current organizational map)

CLARIFY OBJECTIVES
(the strategic management group)

ESTABLISH AN INTEGRATION FRAMEWORK
(the strategic integration group)

DEVISE OPERATIONAL PLAN
(common language)

DEVELOP STAFF
(resourcing development and operation)

IMPLEMENT, MONITOR AND EVALUATE
(expand integration)

Figure 1.2 *Integrating quality and competence – a plan*

There is, therefore, a need for an integrative approach which avoids duplication and reduces complexity. Having tested such an approach with major organizations a plan for this integration has emerged, and is illustrated in Figure 1.2.

CASE STUDY

The following case study illustrates the potential of the integrative approach to quality and competence. It outlines developments in a large manufacturing organization which is undergoing a major change programme. As the long-term plans are still developing, the organization must be referred to as 'Company X'.

Company X is a large manufacturing organization with offices and sites around the world. In one major site, an extensive change programme was stimulated by plans to upgrade plant and equipment. These plans required a complete restructuring of the workforce and new ways of working for the 2000+ employees on site.

Some change initiatives had already begun, including a

Total Quality Management programme; a review of pay and incentive systems; revision of performance appraisal; and BS5750/ISO9000 quality procedures. Investigations had also been conducted into teamworking principles and practice. All of these initiatives led to a great deal of activity as staff were briefed on each development and working groups were involved in various analyses and planning activities.

However, it was soon noted that such activities were leading to circular arguments. Each initiative aimed to achieve its own objectives – but could only contribute to overall business objectives if its results were reviewed in conjunction with the results of other initiatives. In addition there was a 'gap' – the quality initiatives underway focused on 'how' quality would be achieved within the change programme, but not on the 'what', ie, what was it that had to be achieved, by individuals and by teams, in order to meet new business objectives?

A competence-based development programme (see figures 1.3 and 1.4) was therefore introduced, beginning with a senior management workshop to clearly define the key purpose of the business. Employees at all levels were involved in the analysis of functions and the development of competences which incorporated the expectations of performance in the 'new world', introducing the use of new plant, implementing the principles of TQM and operating on BS5750/ISO9000 quality procedure system. New health and safety procedures were also incorporated. This development encouraged ownership and involvement of all employees, managers and union representatives.

The results of the analysis were used in a variety of ways. The identification of individual functions facilitated the agreement of new operational roles (role mapping) for individuals and teams.

A report was prepared indicating how data from the competences project could interlink with that from other initiatives to facilitate solutions to key questions. Figure 1.5 illustrates how each question relating to key objectives can be answered by data from a number of projects.

Having defined role maps, data could then be drawn from major initiatives to inform future operations. This process of continuing future operational structures itself validates the decisions regarding individual and team roles.

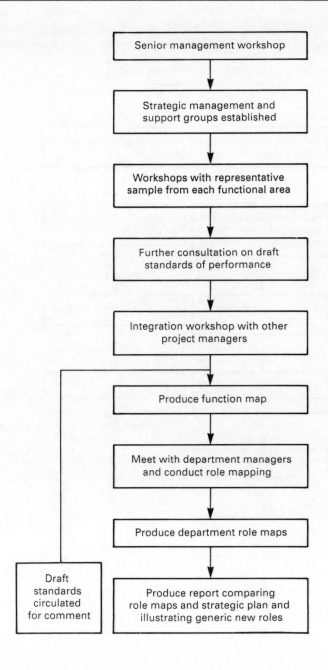

Figure 1.3 *Process for competence-based development programme – phase I*

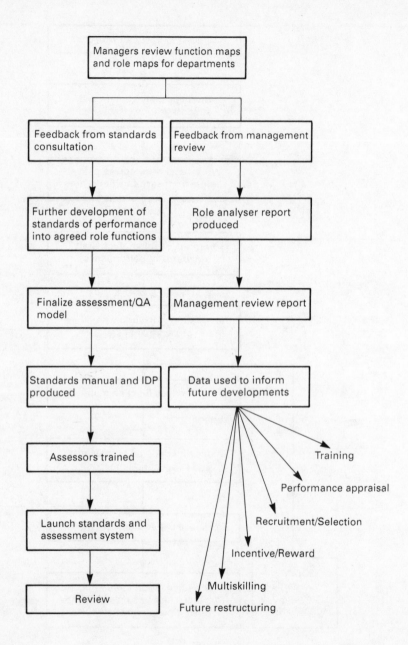

Figure 1.4 *Process for competence-based development – phase II*

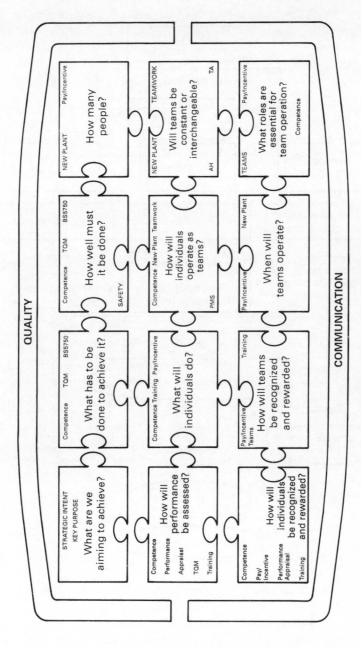

Figure 1.5 *Interlinking of initiatives*

27

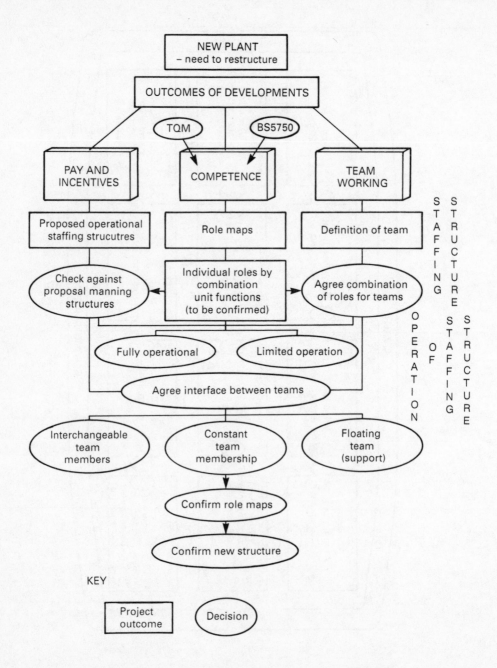

Figure 1.6 *Using the integrative approach for restructuring*

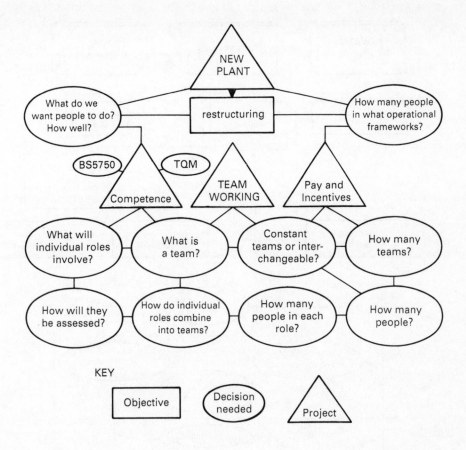

Figure 1.7 *Using the integrative approach to establish team operations*

In this way, the overall process of restructuring (see Figure 1.6), driven by the introduction of new plant and equipment, could be approached on the basis of asking simple, direct questions and drawing data from various initiatives.

Further developments could then take place to establish mechanisms for assessment of performance, recognition of performance, identification of training needs and delivery of targeted training (Figure 1.8).

A role analysis report matches the new roles to existing job descriptions, enabling training gaps and priorities to be identified.

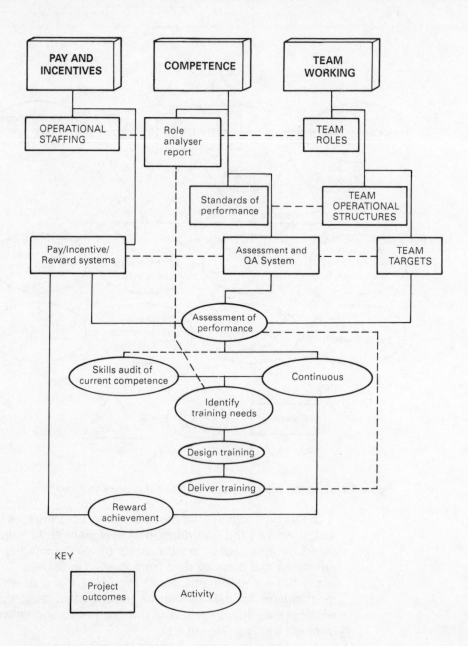

Figure 1.8 *Using the integrative approach to develop assessment, training and incentive strategies*

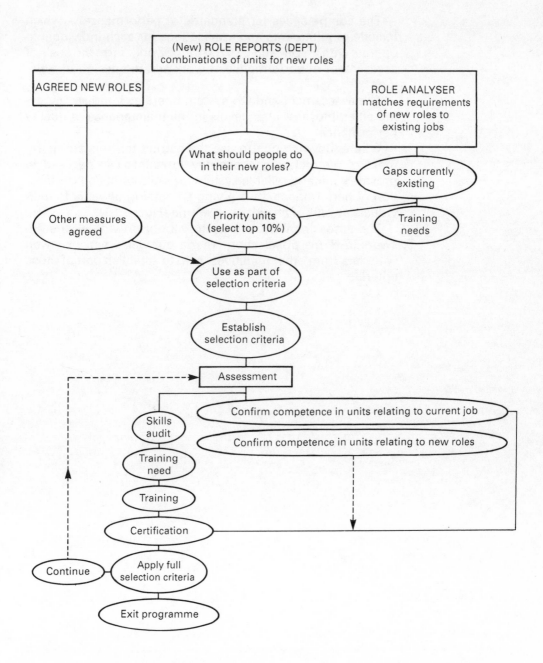

Figure 1.9 *Using the integrative approach in the context of downsizing*

The competences (or standards of performance) – which include requirements and implications for each individual to operate with a TQM and BS5750 framework – form the basis of assessment of performance at work and the design of training.

The assessment and QA system operates in-house involving all employees, at all levels in the maintenance of quality performance.

Where 'downsizing' (to use the current term) is a requirement of restructuring, these developments can be used to provide a fair and reliable system for skills audit and certification of performance, thus giving something of value to individuals as part of an exit programme (Figure 1.9).

The assessment system itself will not provide all the answers in terms of selection criteria but will, when reviewed with data from other initiatives, help to establish part of those criteria.

2 How Might an Integrative Model Work?

▷   SUMMARY   ◁

This chapter:
- reviews some of the most well-known quality initiatives
- outlines areas of overlap and potential duplication of effort
- illustrates how the integration process can be led by the introduction of a competence-based common language

As noted earlier in this book, the term 'quality' is somewhat mysterious – although used extensively, it is not easily defined and we therefore have a plethora of 'quality initiatives' which supposedly aim to improve business performance. In this chapter, I have focused on those quality initiatives which will be most familiar to readers and attempted to illustrate how the integration process can be led by the introduction of a competence-based 'common language'.

Most quality initiatives are introduced because symptoms of lack of quality have been identified – there is a sense that 'things can be run more efficiently'. Often quality is related to 'organizing work' and making sure that everything is done 'right first time'. These two phrases are often used in respect of two of the most common quality initiatives: BS5750 and TQM.

Competence and BS5750/ISO9000

BS5750 and its international counterpart ISO9000 are systems which provide standards of operation, particularly for manufacturing organizations. BS5750 is in three parts:

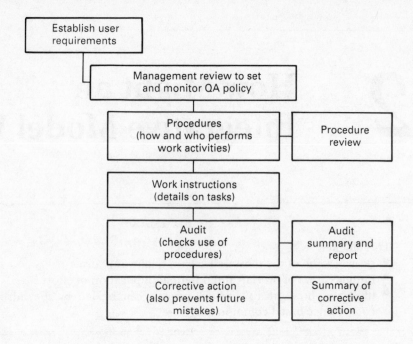

Figure 2.1 *An outline quality assurance system*

- Part One for organizations involved in the design/development, production, installation and servicing of products and services.
- Part Two for organizations making goods or providing services, but not involved in designing or developing those products or services.
- Part Three for organizations which are only involved in inspection and testing.

The development of a BS5750 system begins with a quality policy in a form which everyone can understand. (See pp. 54–62, Chapter 4 for further guidance). It needs to cover who is responsible for the quality assurance system – both setting it up and running it. It needs to express in user-friendly language and in measurable terms, details of how the procedures will be written and reviewed and how failures will be dealt with.

- *A competence-based system requires that mission, values and objectives are expressed in the same way; thus when seeking integration we already have convergence from the top down.*

Procedures

BS5750 requires that procedures are written for the companies' *critical functions*. These will include, among others: assessment, work experience, selection and recruitment, and training and development.

- *As a competence-based system provides the tools, and the basis for all of these activities, we once again have convergence of aims and objectives. A competence-based system defines **what has to be done**; BS5750 procedures will specify **who has to do it (or who is responsible for seeing that it is done)**.*

Work Instructions

As procedures within a BS5750 system are concise, they are usually supported by work instructions (see Figure 2.2). Work instructions refer to one task and provide details on how that task should be completed and therefore provide monitoring for the process of completing a task – competences focus on what has to be achieved and therefore assess competence in achieving the outcome.

Audit

BS5750 requires that an audit is conducted. This relates to auditing of procedures in order to quality assure the processes concerned. Any non-conformance with procedures will be noted and corrective action taken.

- *A competence-based system provides evidence, through continuous assessment of performance, that procedures are being maintained, thus reducing the time needed for auditing. As competence-based assessment is continuous, non-conformance is identified at an early stage and corrective action can be taken immediately. The process of development of competence also identifies where procedures are inadequate or need to be developed in order that evidence of competence can be generated.*

Corrective Action

Corrective action can be explored and decided upon by the operational team in a working context. Within, for example, a BS5750 system, decisions on corrective action will be recorded and procedures amended as necessary.

- *A competence-based system, once operational, utilizes continuous (day-by-day) assessment of workplace performance. If standards within this system reflect the requirements of continuous improvement then the identification and implementation of corrective action is implicit within the workplace performance itself.*

Procedure No. 006

Prior to each and every training event, the trainer responsible for that event will prepare the training room following Work Instruction No. 100.

Check & Comment	Work Instruction No. 100	Standard
	Item	
	• Check floor is clear	N/A
	• Position chairs and tables	As plan
	• Position audio-visual equipment	As plan
	• Check surfaces are free from dust	N/A
	• Test audio-visual equipment	
	– bulbs working	Including spare
	– sound level adequate	Audible at back of room
	– picture quality clear	Visible
	– channel setting correct	Video channel 5
	• Lay out pens and writing	Company headed

Figure 2.2 *Example work instruction*

Integrating Competence and Quality Procedures

A BS5750 quality manual can be developed alongside competences rather than as a separate activity. The quality manual will provide a reference point for monitoring of processes (and for training design), whilst competences will incorporate the critical aspects of quality processes and be used to assess individual and team performance in achieving quality.

Time spent by staff reviewing procedures and writing quality manuals can be aligned with time defining individual standards (or outcomes) of performance.

Competence and Total Quality Management (TQM)

TQM philosophy is based on the assumption that suppliers need both to improve quality and reduce costs in order to survive. TQM consultants will refer to the 'cost of non-quality'.

The quality focus is not simply on products and services, but in all areas of business operation and includes: developing measures of performance, developing a competitive strategy, ensuring effective communication, continuous improvement, and simple procedures for quality performance.

TQM concentrates on an initial top-down approach: the importance of identifying the market correctly – what do the customers want, and who are the customers in the first place?

- *Competence-based systems require a top-down approach and require a well-defined Key Purpose (overall aims and objectives of the business). Competences are explicit and measurable standards of people performance related directly to the business objectives. Competence-based systems incorporate continuous assessment, identification of training needs and of non-conformance. Review of standards is continuous and communication is facilitated by a common language and the establishment of clear communication channels. Moreover, all employees are involved in the system, and are encouraged to take resposibility for their own, and thus the business performance.*

Employee Involvement

TQM utilizes 'quality circles' and 'naturally occurring work teams' to review and report on quality issues.

Quality circles will be well known to many readers as a defined working group which has been set the objective of monitoring and improving quality within their specified work area. Naturally occurring work teams are a development within a continuous improvement programme and refer to working groups formed by members who have frequent business contact on decision-making or process matters on a day-to-day basis.

- *The development of an effective in-company competence-based assessment system should be based on employee involvement and therefore the establishment of ownership. The operation of a competence-based system utilizes assessor networks to monitor quality. Individuals and teams each have details of the standards to be achieved, and opportunities to discuss effects on quality through continuous assessment, feedback and coaching.*

The Issue of Overlap

The brief review of BS5750 and TQM in this chapter outlines some of the overlap and possible duplication of effort that can occur both in the development and implementation of quality systems. The chapter review highlights in table form the areas of overlap (see page 41).

An organization which has both a TQM and BS5750 initiative already has groups of individuals working on very similar tasks, but for different reasons. If a competence-based system is introduced, whether company-specific or a nationally devised scheme, further duplication is created along with confusion of terminology.

Regardless of the state of development of other initiatives, a competence-based approach can provide the 'glue' to bring together the framework for quality. Work on quality manuals covering procedures and on quality measures for processes can be integrated in the central common language of individual and team performance. Quality circles can be utilized to review performance of the team, to exchange ideas and difficulties in operating an assessment system and to encourage and develop a sense of individual responsibility for career planning and development.

In this way, the concepts and principles behind quality initiatives are combined in one central organizational tool. Auditing of quality is also centralized as continuous assessment provides evidence for both individual and business performance.

Involvement of all employees is a component of all three initiatives; the aims of TQM in particular can therefore be achieved by the development of competences for individuals and groups.

Another aim of continuous improvement is achieved through continuous assessment of individual performance. In addition, the TQM objective of encouraging line management to support staff is encompassed in the required performance management role of managers as assessors of day-to-day workplace performance. Managers themselves are also assessed against explicit standards which include the requirement to monitor and measure staff performance.

Developing an Integrative System

By providing a dialogue between planning and action (see Chapter 3), and structuring a framework to support integration (Chapters 4 and 5), the process of development can focus on establishing a common language. This common language can be used for the design of training and development, for performance appraisal, for recruitment and selection.

Activity: create and improve working relationships and practices with team and colleagues

Performance Criteria:

a   Each team member is aware of the contribution they can make to cost-effective operation.
b   Information is complete, accurate, current, recorded and communicated within and between teams.
c   Opportunities for improvement are identified and shared with the team.
d   Methods for prevention of faults are identified and shared with the team and action for improvement implemented.
e   Improvements within line of authority agreed by the team are implemented and communicated to all concerned.
f   Quality targets are available and known by all team members.
g   Operating conditions and information provided on hand-over allow teams taking over an area of work to operate safely, efficiently and cost-effectively.

Range:

Team agreements: Within the scope of agreed team authority.
Operating conditions: Condition of plant and equipment, condition of working environment.
Information: Prevailing condition of plant and equipment, factors affecting, or likely to affect, operations.

Evidence:

Performance: Observation of performance in the workplace.
                Improvements implemented.
                Feedback from colleagues and other teams.
Knowledge: Teamworking and continuous improvement principles and methods of application.

Figure 2.3 *Competence-based standard incorporating 'continuous improvement' and 'teamworking' applications in the workplace*

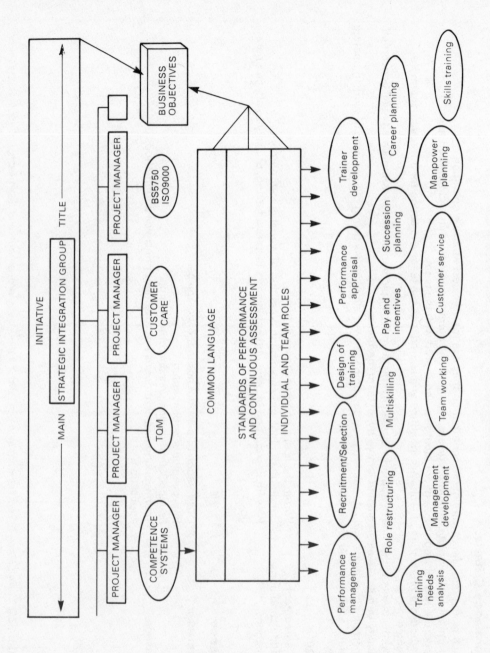

Figure 2.4 *Strategic integration, quality initiatives*

It can be incorporated into performance appraisal systems.

The competence structure and content can incorporate the definition of behaviours and essential terminology required of those people operating within a quality system. For example, Figure 2.3 illustrates one standard expressed in a form to incorporate aspects of teamwork and continuous improvement. (Other examples are provided in later chapters).

Planned changes and new ways of working can be incorporated and the framework itself provides a basis for role-structuring both immediately and in the future. Figure 2.4 illustrates the operative model.

REVIEW			
	Competence	**TQM**	**BS5750**
Teams	develop standards of performance	quality circles resolve non-conformance	prepare quality manuals
Standards	what has to be to be achieved – individual	what has to to be achieved – group, process	who is responsible
Audit	individual	process	procedures
Improvement	continuous assessment of individual performance	continuous improvement culture	continuous monitoring of procedures
	People	**Culture**	**Procedures**

Issue of overlap

Staff time spent on separate activities:
- duplicates effort
- duplicates cost
- creates complexity
- confuses terminology.

Integration:
- avoids duplication/complexity/confusion
- provides a common language for all human resources-related business activities.

3 The Starting Point

▷   SUMMARY   ◁

This chapter:
- explores 'Initiative Overload'
- introduces the first step in the integrative model: Establishing your Starting Point.

Quality and Competence Are Not Mutually Exclusive

In addition to the existence of confusion about the meaning of the terms 'quality' and 'competence', there is a tendency to perceive these two concepts as somehow mutually exclusive.

The first part of this chapter explores this perception and its effect within business organizations. You might like to consider how the issues explored here relate to your own company context – this will help with your research and reporting in Chapter 4.

In reality, approaches to improvement of quality and to improvement of competence can be, and should be, complementary. Any initiative implemented within a company should contribute to the company objectives and encompass the company culture and values. However, this often seems to be far from reality. The right initiatives are often introduced for the wrong reasons.

In practice, many organizations begin the introduction of a range of initiatives and projects, each with its own terminology, its own tools, and usually championed or piloted by one part of the company. This may include 'quality' initiatives such as total quality management (TQM) or continuous improvement (CI), BS5750/ISO9000 (for quality procedures) or 'competence-based' initiatives for assessment and/or training.

Each of these is valuable in its own right and addresses a particular identified need – but it often fails to integrate with, and thus comple-ment, each of the other initiatives instigated by other departments to meet other identified needs. This can lead to a frustrating lack of direc-tion, duplication of effort and increased cost. 'Competing for manage-ment time' becomes increasingly prevalent as each new project holds its seminars and briefings for managers, and as teams apparently duplicate effort.

This type of activity often results in the failure of any quality or competence initiative or project to achieve its objectives – assuming that clear objectives have been established at the outset – and it is surprising how often this is not done, or done half-heartedly.

Planning and Action

It may be stating the obvious, but establishing and achieving clear objec-tives requires planning and action – and it seems that many organizations fail even at this point. Why? Perhaps because the important word in the 'planning and action' phrase, and the one which gets least attention, is 'and'!

I have found that decision-makers around the world often focus on either planning or action rather than recognizing the need to produce a dialogue between the two. This may be due to a number of factors, themselves related to which initiative is uppermost in the company focus at any one time. Each initiative has its own planning mechanism and an established action plan for implementation.

Company actions for change, including the introduction of new qual-ity/competence initiatives, are often influenced by popular trends and the current approach to change management. This may include guid-ance from leading authors on the role of planning and/or action in business improvement strategies. For example, Gerard Egan (1988) sug-gests that planning is 'both essential and dangerous... if the organization does not plan well, change efforts can go off half-cocked'.

If taken literally, this approach can lead to a situation in which plan-ning becomes the norm – and no action results.

EXAMPLE

An organization had been planning its Quality Change Programme for 18 months. Each planning task had been carefully identified and listed; a project planning group met regularly to review the planning task list. The objective was to complete the long list of planning tasks before imple-mentation could take place.

Meanwhile, managers had, over this 18-month period, attended various briefings and planning workshops where they had been asked for opinions and ideas. They were at first enthusiastic, later confused, even later frustrated and finally bored. Why? Because there had been no action.

So perhaps companies should consider other approaches to planning and action for quality and competence? For example Weick (1969) counsels against over-planning: '... planning can insulate members from the very environment which they are trying to cope with.' He also suggests that 'chaotic action is preferable to orderly inaction'.

This proposition is based on the premise that inaction, when reviewed, is puzzling and senseless; when reviewing what hasn't been done, it is more likely that bizarre meanings will be attached. But action provides tangible items that can be reviewed – what I usually refer to as 'having something on the table to work with'. Again, taken literally, this approach can result in lots of action, but no direction.

EXAMPLE

A company wanted to explore how a competence-based framework could be integrated within the planned human resources review and link with its current quality projects. One of my first questions was, 'How many initiatives are operating at present?' No-one was sure, but after investigation it was discovered that there were 18! Each had begun with the intention of improving some aspect of quality business performance, each was based on a particular philosophy, each had its own tools and techniques – but none was integrated. There was no overall plan which brought together the objectives of all these projects.

This chaotic action was beneficial only in creating a sense of 'at least something is happening'. But it was in danger of creating frustration, confusion, boredom and lack of interest or belief that anything was really changing.

Dialogue and Integration

Egan (1988) suggests that what is needed is a dialogue between planning and action: 'action is brash; it usually does not wait for the end of the planning process'. I would like to suggest that this dialogue itself is not sufficient. It must also lead to integration and thus to reduction of complexity and duplication.

By examining the real objectives of the various approaches, initiatives and projects for quality and competence that companies introduce, it is possible to identify common ground and to provide a common language for future action.

The establishment of a common language is central to success. While it may appear a simple and logical step it is one which is rarely taken – especially at the beginning of the planning process. For example, a good indicator of the potential success or failure of a new project is the action which takes place between the first and second planning meetings.

EXAMPLE

An organization asked for tenders for a project to develop a new performance assessment system. I was shown the tender which had been received with most enthusiasm. It included an initial planning meeting to decide what the project objectives were, followed by another planning meeting, one month later, to decide what action was going to be taken. This was to be followed two weeks later by a further meeting to decide who was going to take the action decided upon.

The first question to be asked concerned the organization's preference for this tender. It was discovered that a preference for 'effective planning' existed and therefore this proposal seemed in line with its own management style.

The next question concerned the objectives of the project. Why was it necessary to have an initial meeting to clarify project objectives – had these not been clarified in the original invitation to tender? Why was this project being instigated?

After much discussion, it emerged that no one was really sure why the project had been commissioned or what its real objectives were. Senior management had requested that action be taken to 'improve quality of service' and an invitation to tender had been sent to various consultancies. There was recognition that this project would to some extent overlap with others and some concern that managers would find the duplication of effort frustrating, but this project 'was not exactly the same' as others (which were already underway) and targeted a 'different operational group'.

Several key components were missing in the planning and integration stages of this example – definition of terms, clarification of objectives for the project, integration of this project with others, milestones, targets, deliverables and confirmation of understanding. In short, there was a lack of dialogue between action and planning both for this project and in respect of its integration with any other actions for change.

Initiative Overload Syndrome

This example illustrates how 'competing for management time' is in danger of becoming the phrase of the 1990s. In the drive for quality, it seems that companies forget to take the route map.

Somehow, the use of logic and common sense disappears when it comes to planning and implementing a quality assurance system. Perhaps the consultants do such a convincing job in selling their quality approach, or perhaps the need to compete in a (perceived) quality market is so great that logical thought and simple questioning fly out of the window! Almost without fail, there is an expectation that quality assurance systems, by definition, are complex and therefore require a mystical terminology of their own.

The need to introduce a new initiative of some kind may be stimulated by many events, including a recession, more competitive markets, a drop in sales, change of management .... Whatever the reason, a new initiative seems to be required.

With this decision made, usually a number of meetings follow. Various management groups meet to discuss strategy, to review the mission statement and objectives, to establish new working values and instigate the right culture. Responsibility is delegated, research for the newest and most appropriate approach is instigated.

A number of scenarios may then take place (are any of them familiar to you?).

- Scenario 1 – Gain support by championing. Each person conducting research attempts to gain support for their preferred initiative – a champion system emerges. Someone, preferably at director level, has to be convinced that *this* initiative is the one that has real value.
- Scenario 2 – Throw money at it. Everything can be solved if enough money is made available. The more it costs the better the quality must be.
- Scenario 3 - Find the cheapest route. Each researcher has to find the most efficient and most cost-effective route to improving quality – the best cases get the budget.

Every possible new approach is investigated. Recommendations and costings are produced and reproduced. More meetings follow; costings are reviewed. Those who are responsible for existing initiatives see their budgets about to be cut in favour of something new. Future initiative 'champions' begin to plan, calculating the number of new staff they will need; working out how to spend their budget; and preparing briefings for senior management.

This round of activity can take up to two years in a single, multinational organization. The management group becomes caught in the planning phase – a dialogue of planning and action does not exist, so nothing happens to improve the situation that was so urgent in the first place.

A key outcome of scenarios such as these is 'initiative overload'.

Initiative overload is a useful tool for solving problems through creating confusion. This is a fairly recent phenomenon, the syndrome perhaps being brought on by the need to respond to a difficult world recession.

Many companies have had to face up to the need for redundancies. To cope with this unpleasant change, there is a need to become convinced that the new structure will improve overall business operation and therefore business performance. We therefore find companies centralizing or decentralizing operations; we find management structures changing to flatter hierarchies and teams; we find cultures changing to consultative, or the development of a learning organization.

However, rather than addressing a real problem, we often find that the key stimulus for this exciting new initiative is expressed as the need to establish/maintain an image of being at the leading edge of the newest developments. Thus, there is often a reluctance to acknowledge the real issue and a general tendency to replace it with exciting new initiatives. This approach creates two new problems: a) no one sorts out the real problem and b) there are so many initiatives that no one understands (or is motivated by) any of them.

Identifying the Starting Point

To go forward, one needs a starting point – and it is this which causes many companies so much difficulty. One simple question puts this into focus – 'Why?' Why do you need to improve training? Why do you think your TQM programme is not working? Why have you decided that you need a management development programme?

Decisions regarding the need for various initiatives are often based on paper-thin criteria – the phrase, 'it seemed like a good idea at the time' usually springs to mind. Tracing back the origin of these decisions often leads us to the view that this approach happens to be somebody's favourite (perhaps because they experienced it somewhere else), or a consultant did a pretty good job of convincing the management team that they couldn't do without this one.

The next question to ask is 'How will this initiative fit with others currently operating within the company?'. You will either be snowed under by terminology, photocopies of handouts and explanations of

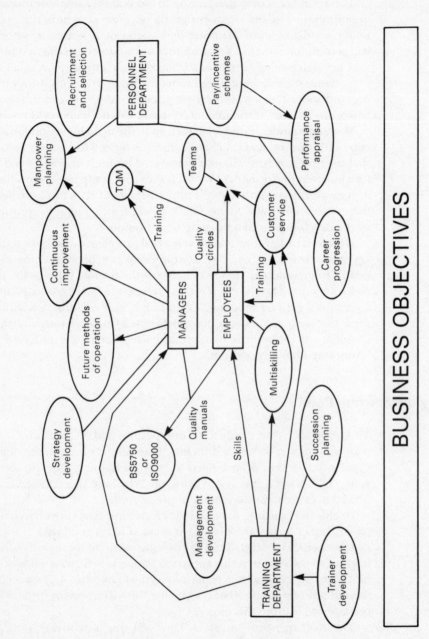

Figure 3.1 *Initiative overload syndrome*

concepts, or you will be met with a blank stare. Either way, your question is unlikely to be answered.

It is at this point that we begin to recognize the symptoms of Initiative Overload Syndrome. This is a state of play within a company in which several different games are underway and no one knows the rules of any of them. Figure 3.1 illustrates this syndrome and the chaos that can be caused as different departments and occupational groups attempt to communicate with each other and to implement the project outcomes within various business activities.

Taking the First Step

By recognizing and acknowledging these symptoms we have the opportunity to begin the journey back to common sense and simplicity – if the questions about fitting together various initiatives can be taken seriously.

We begin the journey by establishing our starting point and in the company context this means identifying the following:

- How many initiatives are currently operating?
- What are their objectives?
- Who is responsible for their management?

These may seem to be very simple questions – even quite obvious – but it is surprising how often the obvious is missed. Even identifying *how many* initiatives are operating can be a problem – due to delegated responsibility, pilot activity and what is actually understood by the term 'initiative'.

For our purposes, we will assume that an 'initiative' includes any project (current or planned) which aims to improve an aspect of business performance. This may include major quality or competence programmes, or the development of a new incentive system, or a new performance appraisal system, or the redesign of the training function.

The answer to the third question depends of course on the answers to the first two – unless one knows how many projects are running, one is unlikely to know who is managing them. Managers at all levels are surprised to find out just how many initiatives are operating within one company – and they are even more surprised to discover the duplication of effort that is involved.

This then is the Initiative Overload Syndrome – 'new and exciting projects, initiatives and pilots' operating throughout the company. Duplication of effort (and cost). Competition for management time as managers attend various training programmes and seminars. In general, a lack of direction – brought about by dismissal of the obvious, lack of

```
┌─────────────────────────────────────────────────────────┐
│        ┌───────────────────────────────────────┐        │
│        │      ESTABLISH STARTING POINT          │        │
│        │    (the current organizational map)    │        │
│        └───────────────────────────────────────┘        │
│                                                         │
│                   CLARIFY OBJECTIVES                     │
│              (the strategic management group)            │
│                                                         │
│          ESTABLISH AN INTEGRATION FRAMEWORK              │
│              (the strategic integration group)           │
│                                                         │
│                 DEVISE OPERATIONAL PLAN                  │
│                   (a common language)                    │
│                                                         │
│                    DEVELOP STAFF                         │
│           (resourcing development and operation)         │
│                                                         │
│           IMPLEMENT, MONITOR AND EVALUATE                │
│                  (expand integration)                    │
│                                                         │
└─────────────────────────────────────────────────────────┘
```

Figure 3.2 *Step 1 – establish the starting point*

coordination and failure to identify the real starting point.

You might like to check if this situation exists in your own company. This is the first step in the integrative plan, as illustrated in Figure 3.2. Two tasks follow to help you take this first step.

The first step is to identify your starting point and map the organizational position of current and planned initiatives and projects.

Try the following simple exercise. It may take some time, but it may also provide some valuable insight into your own organization's direction for the future. It will also provide the basis for further activities in later chapters.

Task 1 – Survey

Prepare a questionnaire as illustrated below and issue it to colleagues and managers to complete.

Please answer each question as fully as possible;

The company has/is running a number of initiatives/projects which involve staff in attending training programmes, seminars or workshops. Each of these initiatives is an action for change.

1. Please list below the initiatives/projects you are aware of:

2. Please list those you are involved in:

3. For each initiative/project you have included in (1) and (2) above, please provide the following information on a separate sheet.

What are its aims and objectives?

When did it start?

When will it finish?

How will it change what you do?

How will it improve work for you?

Who manages it?

How much time have you spent working on it

in training programmes?

in seminars?

in workshops?

in team activities (please specify)?

in other activities?

CHECK YOUR RESULTS

Questions 1 and 2 Did people write the full name of the project or just the acronym?

Were the lists in 1 and 2 the same?

How many were listed?

Did managers list more than other colleagues?

Question 3 How many people know start and finish dates?

How many reacted positively to how it would change their work?

How many reacted positively to how it would improve work for them?

How many know who the project manager is?

What is the total time people have spent on each project?

How much duplication of activity does there seem to be?

These are just some of the questions you might consider. The information collected in this short survey is very valuable. It tells you something about your company's sense of direction, about the effectiveness of its communication, about the integration of various projects and initiatives, about the motivation and reaction of staff.

If there are comments or indications that too much time is spent on these projects so 'we can't get our work done', then these are probably symptoms of initiative overload.

Task 2 – Mapping

If you find that initiative overload does exist, you can first provide data to make appropriate people aware of its existence. You can then begin to take action to resolve it.

- Collate the information you have obtained from your survey.
- List the initiatives identified by the people surveyed.
- Follow up to identify the following:
  - What is the title of the project/initiative?
  - What are its objectives?
  - Who is managing it?
  - When did it start?
  - When will it finish?

Note any difficulties in obtaining this information, any gaps in the information and any discrepancies you may identify. Compile this information into a simple matrix format as in the example in Figure 3.3.

When you have completed this task, you will have probably the first map of current initiatives and projects produced for your company. You can now begin to identify areas of overlap between objectives and check how these projects do (or don't) fit together to make a cohesive whole.

project title	objectives	comm.	end	manager
TQM	establish cooperative culture and teamwork	2/92	2/93	J.Smith
BS5750	quality manual	4/92	10/92	B.Brown
CI	teamwork	6/92	7/93	H.Black
Performance Appraisal	new assessment scheme	3/92	9/92	G.Green
Competence	qualifications/assessment	8/92	8/93	H.Jones
Project Blue	customer interaction	2/92	? ?	
Competence	developing training	6/92	12/92	Training dept.
Quality circles	product quality	9/92	4/93	Personnel

Figure 3.3 *Mapping matrix*

The map you have produced provides the basis on which further research and planning and action can progress – remembering that it is the dialogue between planning and action and the integration of initiatives that is your objective.

REVIEW

Planning and action require dialogue.
Dialogue should lead to integration.
Step 1: Identify the starting point
- Identify symptoms of initiative overload:
  - competition for management time;
  - confusion;
  - frustration;
  - lack of clarity of project objectives.
- Identify your company starting point:
  - how many initiatives?
  - what objectives?
  - who is responsible?
- Produce your mapping matrix.

4 The Framework for Integration – Researching and Reporting

> SUMMARY <

This chapter:
- helps you to begin the preparation of a report or presentation for your next line manager to progress, or for the senior management group itself, in which you can outline the information you have collected, the need to integrate, the benefits of integration, plus an initial action plan.

ESTABLISH STARTING POINT
(the current organizational map)

CLARIFY OBJECTIVES
(the strategic management group)

ESTABLISH AN INTEGRATION FRAMEWORK
(the strategic integration group)

DEVISE OPERATIONAL PLAN
(a common language)

DEVELOP STAFF
(resourcing development and operation)

IMPLEMENT, MONITOR AND EVALUATE
(expand integration)

Figure 4.1 *Clarifying the objectives*

Preparing the Ground

Task 3 – The Outline of Your Report

If you have completed the two tasks in the previous chapter, you will now be in possession of some very valuable information – its value particularly relating to its potential use as the basis for an organizational tool.

In order to implement this, the senior management group must first be aware of the information you have collated and of its importance.

You may have found that your organization is operating, or planning, a number of initiatives in respect of 'quality' eg TQM, BS5750, ISO9000, Continuous Improvement. You may have some form of 'competence' initiative underway – eg competence-based standards linked to a national qualification system, assessment centres, a new performance appraisal system.

The senior management group will need a briefing on your findings and some suggestions on what needs to happen next. The following questions will help you to prepare for this; the other chapters in this book will provide you with further help. First, consider these questions:

- What is the key importance of competent performance of employees in our organization?
- What is the cost of failure in our organization?
- How does competent performance directly link with our view of quality?
- Do we have a quality policy and/or strategy?

When you have considered these questions, you should then note your ideas on the importance of integration of quality and competence initiatives for your organization. These might include:

- cost of failure
- avoiding duplication of effort
- avoiding duplication of cost
- achievement of company mission and objectives
- improvement in communication

You should note your initial comments, based on the data you have collected from your survey (see previous chapter). Your briefing to the management group, whether undertaken as a presentation or in a written report, should answer all the questions and address the key issues noted above.

At this point you are not required to provide the ultimate solution in the form of a detailed plan of action. Your aim is to help the management group recognize the value of adopting an integrated approach (see Chapter 1) in your own organizational context in order that action can be taken. This begins the dialogue between planning and action and also begins to establish the framework for integration.

Task 4 – Research

You now need to undertake some detailed research and identify some key policies and strategies.

One of the first items you will need to identify is the *company quality policy*. This is a key component of a quality assurance system – but not all organizations have them. If your company has BS5750 or ISO9000 accreditation, it will have a quality policy document which should meet the criteria listed in Figure 4.2. If you find that your organization doesn't have a quality policy note this as the first action point in your report.

A quality policy should include:
- details of functions for which quality procedures will be/are defined;
- details of review procedures;
- details of monitoring procedures;
- details of how failures will be rectified;
- who is responsible for
    a) setting up
    b) monitoring
    the system.

The quality policy should also be:
- easy to understand;
- accessible;
- specific.

Figure 4.2 *Quality policy checklist*

The Quality Strategy

Policies must be put into action – which requires a plan or strategy. You now need to research your company strategy. To do so, you will need to collect information from various sources as many people can be involved in operating a strategy.

You might start by finding out if there is a strategic document (and whether you can have access to it). As you collect and review the documents relating to the strategy and its implementation, there are a number of key ideas to keep in mind – or rather to help you keep an open mind! People tend to be overawed by something as impressive as a strategy, and can get engrossed in the words rather than seeing past them to their meaning.

Read the following section on the Strategic Orchestra before beginning your research. It outlines a situation which is very common in companies around the world – and it may help you to review your own organizational context with an objective viewpoint.

The Strategic Orchestra

Companies plan strategically to improve quality. This activity usually takes some time. It produces policies and proposed proceedings, even a detailed scheme – but it doesn't, of itself, result in any action. Strategies can look marvellous, but someone has to make them come alive. This can be a difficult task as, quite often, strategic planning is bound up in terminology that no one really understands such as:

organization development;	organization dynamic;
strategy formulation;	dynamic strategy;
strategic planning;	learning strategy;
strategic intent;	managing vs directing;
crafting strategy;	management vs manager;
intrapreneurship;	business dynamic.

The outcomes of strategic planning on quality issues are often displayed in company reception areas and around the company's offices. They are usually presented on huge notice boards in main areas and in nicely framed presentations around managers' work areas. They usually include statements such as:

OUR QUALITY MISSION
OUR QUALITY VALUES
OUR QUALITY VISION

They look very impressive and everyone is frequently asked to quote them – but what do they actually mean? Where do they come alive within the company?

The drive for quality gets underway with this display of vision and values – everyone has faithfully learned the company vision, mission and values off by heart and is aware that exciting things are about to happen. No one is quite sure yet exactly what these exciting things are, but a budget has been allocated so it must be true.

The detailed scheme prepared by the strategic planning group probably contains a (secret) budget figure and a number of objectives. Action to achieve these objectives is usually delegated through several levels of management and each level begins its own planning phase. However, in this process of delegation and further forward planning, the importance of upward and lateral communication somehow gets lost.

Further rounds of reading and planning at last result in action. Personnel begins a review of remuneration systems. The training department (if it still exists), examines the new training policy and reorganizes its resources. The new quality assurance department sets a group to work on writing a quality manual while someone, somewhere, works on a new performance appraisal system.

Meanwhile the strategic management group meets to review operations and consider a restructuring programme based on consultant recommendations for methods of operation and a customer survey is launched in order to establish the 'optimum client interface' and perhaps provide the foundation for a major customer service employee development programme – aimed to improve the quality of customer service.

We also find that the individual employee has not been forgotten in this arena of new initiatives. The new remuneration system is to be linked to achievement of new competence-based qualifications which are to be introduced to all roles over the next three years. This will provide a further incentive for improved performance and provide each individual with explicit standards of performance against which they can be assessed by their line manager.

This scenario might be compared to one in which a dozen orchestras are playing in one place – this might be quite an achievement and quite enjoyable if it weren't for the fact that each is playing a different tune!

Figure 4.3 provides a real-life example of a strategic orchestra in action – the context is simply referred to as Company X,

Task 5 – Map your Orchestra

If you completed the activity in Task 1, you might like to set out your findings in a similar diagram. Many companies could produce a chart like this which shows an amazing number of people undertaking an amazing number of activities with none of them coordinated; and yet they all started from the same sheet music – didn't they? They all read the strategic document, they all rehearsed and learned the mission and

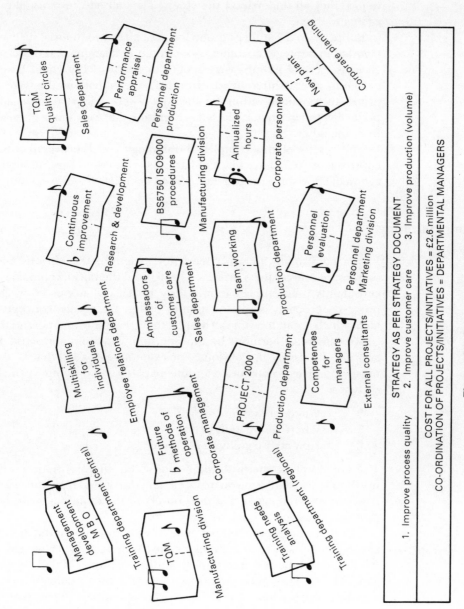

Figure 4.3 *Strategic orchestra in action*

values, they all understood the vision. They all had responsibility delegated to them.

But perhaps the strategy group forgets one or two things – such as the fact that its strategic document was written in a language it understood (because several months were spent discussing it) but could be interpreted in several different ways by others. Or perhaps all the issues and proposals contained within the documents were delegated to the appropriate division or branch without recognition that each works in isolation from the other.

The results of this complex terminology and the overall strategic approach often include a lack of harmony, confusion, frustration, duplication of effort and cost and the creation of initiative overload syndrome.

Creating Harmony

I have consistently found a tendency to ignore the obvious and to overcomplicate business process. Throughout the world, companies and consultants use complex terminology to 'tag' what can be a simple process – probably because it sounds better. We dismiss concepts and ideas which seem 'too simple' despite their real value and potential.

We can create harmony by applying simplicity, common sense, logic and not dismissing the obvious. For example, if I say 'What is usually missing in many companies is a route map' – based on simple principles such as:

- Where are we now?
- Where do we want to go?
- How are we going to get there?

This could well be met with the response 'but that's obvious, everyone needs to know that!' But you may well have discovered from the tasks you have already completed that the answers to these questions are not as obvious as one might easily assume.

The three simple questions can themselves form the foundation for a strategic approach to integrating quality. Your work so far on Tasks 1-5 has addressed the first question. If you have completed these tasks you should have a fairly good picture of where your organization is now. The mapping matrix from the previous chapter and your 'strategic orchestra' diagram from this one will provide you with some powerful visual aids within your report or presentation.

Similarly, your review of strategy should have given some indication at least (depending on how good the strategy is), of where your organization is going. This too can be presented in your report in terms of key objectives of the company and the 'route map' planned to achieve them.

But your report is incomplete. The facts and figures you already have need to be combined with more specific information about objectives and this can only be done by the management group.

The next steps in the model can therefore be implemented when this information has been collected. So what needs to happen next? Let's go back to our plan.

ESTABLISH STARTING POINT
(the current organizational map)

CLARIFY OBJECTIVES
(the strategic management group)

ESTABLISH AN INTEGRATION FRAMEWORK
(the strategic integration group)

DEVISE OPERATIONAL PLAN
(a common language)

DEVELOP STAFF
(resourcing development and operation)

IMPLEMENT, MONITOR AND EVALUATE
(expand integration)

Figure 4.4 *Steps 2 and 3 – the framework*

Your report now provides feedback from your research, but needs to outline what must happen to begin the dialogue of planning and action and achieve integration. The senior management group will have to take the next steps. It will need your ideas on what these next steps should be.

You can progress these next steps by outlining a structure which will facilitate the integration process. This structure is illustrated in the next chapter.

REVIEW

Your outline report:
1. Project map (see Chapter 2).
2. Need for integration (related to your organization's context).
3. Identify company quality policy.
4. Research company strategy.
5. Map your organization's strategic orchestra.
6. Present for review and consideration of further action (Chapter 5).

Reminders – Remember to keep a dialogue of planning and action
Top down commitment is essential
Next step – Outline the structure of working groups to facilitate integration

5 The Integration Framework

> SUMMARY <

This chapter:
* helps you to finish your initial report by including some recommendations for action to establish the framework required to operate the integrative model.

ESTABLISH STARTING POINT
(the current organizational map)

CLARIFY OBJECTIVES
(the strategic management group)

ESTABLISH AN INTEGRATION FRAMEWORK
(the strategic integration group)

DEVISE OPERATIONAL PLAN
(a common language)

DEVELOP STAFF
(resourcing development and operation)

IMPLEMENT, MONITOR AND EVALUATE
(expand integration)

Figure 5.1 *Establishing an integration framework*

It is assumed that your report will be presented to the senior management group, which for our purposes will become known as the strategic management group.

The Strategic Management Group

The strategic management group will consist of senior managers who have information regarding company mission, objectives, strategy and policy. Their role in the integration process will be one of guidance at policy level. They will be the decision-makers and will need to review your report. Your initial report should therefore clearly outline who you feel should be a member of this group and the tasks this group will need to undertake.

The three tasks this group will need to undertake are outlined below and must be completed at the beginning of the integration process, followed by policy/budgetary support for the development and implementation phase. Remember – top-down commitment is essential. The strategic management group will therefore need a clear guide on what its tasks will be.

Strategic management group – Task 1

- Agree a common and workable understanding of the company mission, objectives, values and standards

Strategic management group – Task 2

- Clarify objectives

Strategic management group – Task 3

- Answer clearly the question: Where are we going?

Task 1 – Agreeing a Common and Workable Understanding of the Company Mission, Objectives, Values and Standards

The important words associated with the first task are 'common' and 'understandable'.

Many mission statements will be open to interpretation, as will company values – and yet the mission and values should be clear and understood by all employees. (Remember the strategic orchestra in Chapter 4).

The Problem with Standards

The term 'standards' also presents a difficult problem – and opens up the debate about the meaning of standards and also about the role of competent employees. The group should explore what is understood by this term. Does it mean technical standards in manuals, or even procedures as reflected in quality manuals? Are we talking about actual *performance* and, if so, is this performance related to teams or to individuals or to processes or to departments?

If you have completed the research activities outlined earlier in this book, your report will adequately inform the group on this issue, particularly in respect of the importance of competent employees, and the initiatives currently underway or planned, to tackle this issue.

Defining a Clear Mission Statement

For further action, the mission statement and objectives must be expressed in a form which can be easily communicated. Once defined and clearly understood, the mission statement provides (or should provide) an answer to the question 'Where are we going?' The following checklist can provide a basis on which such statements can be prepared.

▷   CHECKLIST   ◁

The mission statement of a company should include all important aspects of the company's future direction. The following is proposed by Ashridge Strategic Management Centre as a checklist for Good Mission Statements:

1. Purpose
Does the statement describe an inspiring purpose that avoids playing to the selfish interests of the stakeholders, shareholders, customers, employees, suppliers?

Does the statement describe the company's responsibility to its stakeholders?

2. Strategy
Does the statement define a business domain, explaining why it is attractive?

Does the statement describe the strategic positioning that the company prefers in a way that helps to identify the sort of competitive advantage it will look for?

3. Values
Does the statement identify values that link with the organization's purpose and act as beliefs that employees can feel proud of?

Do the values resonate with and reinforce the organization's strategy?

4. Behaviour standards
Does the statement describe important behaviour standards that serve as beacons of the strategy and the values?

Are the behaviour standards described in a way that enables individual employees to judge whether they have behaved correctly or not?

5. Character
Does the statement give a portrait of the company capturing the culture of the organization?

Is the statement easy to read?

Source: *Do You Need a Mission Statement?* Campbell and Young, 1990, Economist Publications.

This checklist probably seems rather daunting – especially when many companies think of mission statements as being only one or two sentences long! However, it does illustrate that the mission statement should reflect all aspects of the company operation, including its focus on values as living components of achieving the mission.

Clarifying Values
The strategic management group's review of company mission and values may well identify one of these values as a statement along the lines of 'People are our most valuable resource'.

Early discussions throughout the company will have stressed the importance of this – but where is it reflected in the various initiatives that are taking place? There may be a review of pay and incentive schemes and personnel policies – but does this reflect the stated value of the importance of people, or is it simply a necessity?

Task 2 – Clarify Objectives

Integrating quality requires a people-centred approach – it therefore requires that the stated company values become living values and not simply statements which look good in a frame on office walls.

This key point is illustrated when the group first identifies the gap in its previous planning activities. Few mission statements or identified objectives actually include anything to do with the people who are so valuable to the success of the company.

The Gap in Quality Planning
Strategic thinking and planning for quality often stops at total quality programmes – the name implies it covers everything – or companies recognize that BS5750 or ISO9000 provide the accreditation needed to be recognized as a quality provider. Other initiatives are then seen as contributing to quality – through customer service or general skills

training. Those relating to personnel issues (performance appraisal, pay and incentives, etc) are seen as a separate matter, whilst future methods of operation are yet another issue.

This fragmented thinking and planning encourages the development of initiative overload and all the unnecessary complexity, cost and frustration that goes with it. The gap in thinking arises because people issues, in particular, are seen as isolated issues, not as a vital component of achieving quality in its broad sense.

These components all need to be integrated – and linked to business objectives and values. Figure 5.2 illustrates the link between the people based approach and two of the most common quality initiatives

We can see from Figure 5.2 how a gap in quality planning can arise. If there is a focus on TQM – which centres on culture, and services – and on BS5750 or ISO9000 – which centre on procedures and processes – we are only covering two of the three key components of business success.

TQM concepts must be put into practice by people; quality procedures must be operated by people. To do this, people need to know what they are expected to do and how well they must do it; they need standards of performance.

Task 3 – Where Are We Going?

The strategic management group therefore needs to begin the provision of a framework by adopting a top-down approach and establishing a mission or key purpose for the company which includes its commitment to a people-centred approach. Once this is in place, the framework can be built, ensuring that all its component parts contribute directly to this key purpose.

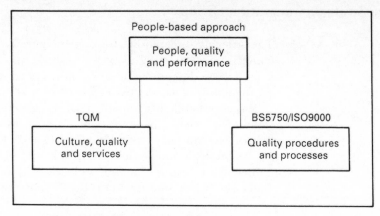

Figure 5.2 *An integrated approach*

The group must, however, establish its mission statement or key purpose in complete and measurable terms. Being measurable is very important, otherwise how will anyone know when objectives have been achieved?

The following will be of help – try testing your own company mission statement and objectives against these key points:

Does the mission statement:

- Describe the key purpose of the company in plain English?
- Define the business domain clearly?
- Identify agreed values?
- Describe important behaviour standards?
- Is it easy to read?

Are the business objectives:

- Expressed in the same language as the mission statement?
- Measurable?
- Achievable within a specified time frame?
- Comprehensive in relation to the mission statement?

Providing a route map

Once the strategic management group has begun these tasks, plans and action (remember the dialogue) for establishing a clear and integrated map of the route to achieve change can be instigated.

This will require the identification of the next level of operation in the integrative model (see Figure 5.1).

The Strategic Integration Group

The strategic integration group (see Figure 2.4, page 40) will usually comprise departmental managers – those who can allocate staff time, brief staff on developments and monitor progress. This group may take on an identity of its own, perhaps becoming known as the 'change team'.

It is essential that the members of this group have a common understanding of the company mission and objectives; the strategic management group must have completed its tasks and communicated the results.

The strategic integration group will be responsible for drawing together all the various strands of project activity into a coherent plan – one which can be communicated to all staff, one which highlights and avoids possible areas of duplicated effort and cost, and one which makes everyone's roles clear. No simple task – but an essential one. So time must be allocated for this team to do its work. If departmental managers cannot be released, then full-time staff need to be appointed – staff with the authority to call upon departmental managers to make staff available.

We now begin to see why top-down commitment is essential: time must be allocated to development; someone, somewhere, has to be responsible. As the strategic integration group draws together all the strands of new developments, they begin to create a framework for change.

Clarify the Route Map

The strategic integration group is now ready to build a framework for change. All the information about current initiatives and projects must be collated and built into a cohesive whole. Each initiative must be reviewed with the strategic and policy issues shown in Figure 5.3 in mind.

- Contribution to improvement of company performance.
- Interface with other quality initiatives.
- Effect on other HR activities.

Figure 5.3 *Strategic and policy issues*

Each project must be reviewed in terms of its outcomes – and the contribution of those outcomes to the agreed mission. Its interface with other initiatives must be established together with its effect on other company operations. Your own work in this area provides the basis for the strategic integration group to put 'flesh on the bones'.

For example, the strategic integration group needs to explore in detail how TQM affects standards of performance for individuals or how a new performance appraisal system might link with training and development or career or succession planning.

The group will need to ensure that it has all necessary information from the people who have responsibility for each project. The group's activities will therefore follow this sequence:

---

1. Review information collated on current/planned projects.
2. Meet with project managers to clarify for each project:
   – objectives;
   – costs;
   – timescales;
   – project management team;
   – link with other projects;
   – impact on other projects;
   – impact on other HR activities.
3. Request from each project manager a report outlining:
   – project plan;
   – timescales and milestones;
   – detailed breakdown of costs;
   – objectives and outcomes;
   – link with other projects.

If you have included all of your research in your report, the strategic integration group will have a sound basis on which to work and will only need to fill in any gaps regarding projected costings or other planned projects.

The reports from this activity can be mapped on charts to illustrate the framework. The charts may look like the example below:

MISSION STATEMENT

To be recognised as the No.1 product leader in the UK and Europe with superior customer service and excellence of staff competence.

Key Objectives	1 Develop New Products	2 Meet Customer Needs	3 Achieve Corporate Learning Culture	4 Improve Marketing Strategy	5 Maintain Consistency in quality of products
Project Title					
1. TQM		Establish customers within the quality process	Establish corporate culture		Improve quality processes
2. BS5750		Review customer needs in defining products			Improve quality procedures
3. Competence		Define standards of performance for all employees	Establish learning/ training needs and continuous assessment		Relate individual performance directly to business objectives
4. Benchmarking	Establish trends			Establish trends	
5. Teamworking		Agree team roles, structures and standards	Establish operational teams		Agree team processes
6.					
7.					
8.					

This charting provides a visual check on all activities for change, and a basis for mapping overlapping objectives, duplication of costs, conflicting activities and gaps in planning.

It may result in some projects being dropped altogether and others being modified as the framework takes place.

Filling the People Gap

Once the charts of existing and planned activities is complete, the gaps can be addressed. It is most likely that the people and standards gap will be most evident and this aspect will need to be addressed immediately.

It is at this point that a competence-based system comes into its own. Its objective is to provide explicit and measurable standards which can give companies a common language from which to build all human resource (ie, people-related) operations. Figure 5.4 illustrates how competence-based standards make performance management a much simpler and logically based operation.

The Need for a Common Language

For these standards of performance to be of real benefit, however, they must relate directly to the mission statement – and if they relate to the

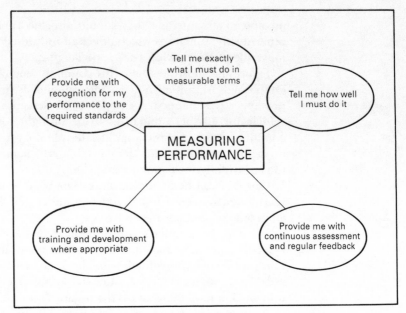

Figure 5.4 *Measuring performance*

71

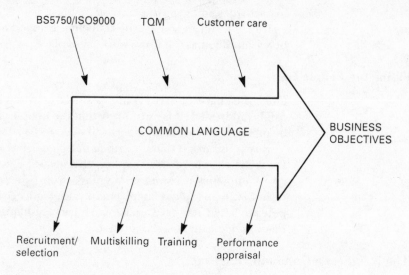

Figure 5.5 *A common language*

mission statement then they should also incorporate those aspects of other quality initiatives which affect an individual's performance. They must, therefore, provide a common language.

Figure 5.5 illustrates how this common language approach can be established. All initiatives are reviewed, and their contribution to business objectives mapped. A competence-based approach then provides a vehicle for all these initiatives to be brought together and ensure a common sense of direction. The terminology from each initiative is incorporated into specific standards of performance for each individual, thus providing one common language.

Once established, this common language is used as the basis for recruitment and selection, design of training, performance appraisal and all people-related business activities.

Because the standards are developed by the company and for the company, and are collated in a way which identifies key components or *functions* of each individual's role, the analysis which leads to the standards development is itself a valuable tool for role restructuring and for information modelling across the organization.

A competence-based approach, if used in an organizational perspective, can therefore provide a company with a powerful management tool,

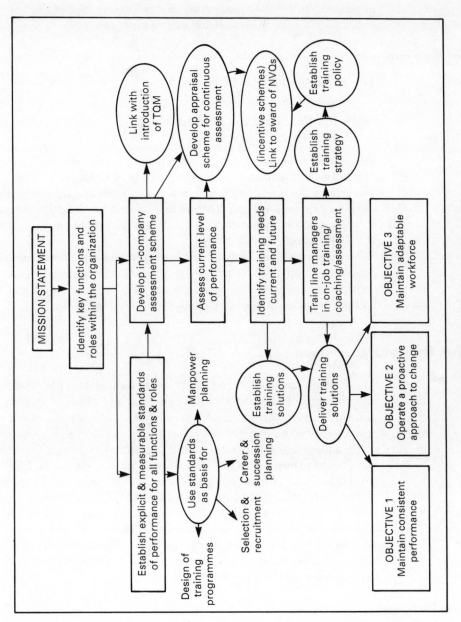

Figure 5.6 *A foundation for improvement*

in addition to meeting the gap created by current lack of explicit standards of performance for individuals and for teams.

Building the Framework

Any framework for change needs at least three major components:

- a clear direction
- central control and management
- effective communication.

The first of these should be provided by the clarification and agreement of a mission statement – or the key purpose of a company – this should also answer the question of 'where are we going?' The second deals with 'how do we get there?' and 'how are we progressing?' The third should be a component of any project if ownership, involvement and commitment (OIC) are to be generated.

Having established the strategic integration group, identified existing projects and initiatives and agreed on a need for a common language, the central management framework can now become operational and begin an effective programme for change throughout the company.

Establish Central Management

The strategic integration group, armed with the data it has collected on all existing projects, needs to draw together all strands of existing work and thus ensure that progress is monitored, duplication avoided and a common direction maintained.

By adopting the role of a central management group, the strategic integration group needs to establish communication channels for each project to report. Clear roles and responsibilities need to be established.

For each individual project (competence, TQM, ISO9000) a project manager must be identified. Each project manager requires adequate support and authority to access resources. In return, each project manager should provide a detailed project plan which includes all components outlined on page 70. Lines of reporting and frequency of progress reports must also be clarified.

Chart the Direction

The data collected from each project manager needs to be compiled into a simple, diagrammatic format. Figure 5.7 might be used as an example – the simpler the better.

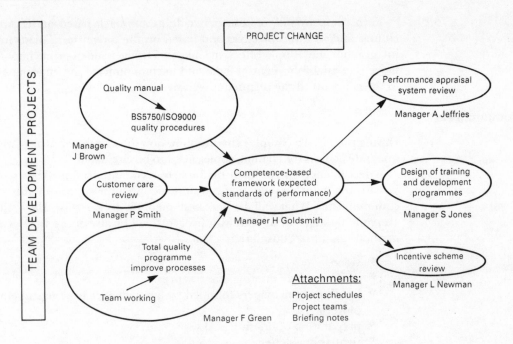

Figure 5.7 *The route map (all initiatives)*

Decide on a Name

I am currently working with one international company which undertook its review of current projects and initiatives to find it had 17 different projects underway. Employees were confused and frustrated by terminology, by time allocated to different projects and by the apparent lack of direction.

By undertaking the initial review, the company was able to identify areas of overlap and duplication of cost and to plan an effective change programme. In order to bring clarity and commitment to this change, all initiatives were grouped under one project title. Employees only have one 'trend' or 'project' to remember, all actions for change are brought together and a sense of direction is generated. The project name should be simple.

Generate a Sense of Importance

A key point is that an integrative project of this kind has enormous potential for change. Many companies which have recognized this have felt that such potential should be communicated with a sense of importance. Thus, some have organized a major launch, with videos, conferences, briefings, and in one case even fireworks and music.

Each company will, of course, decide its approach based on its own culture and its own objectives and based on the longer-term plans for integration (see 'Ripple Effect' in Chapter 7). The issue of prime importance is to establish a central focus and to communicate the importance to the company of the planned integrative project.

Communicate

Having prepared a (simple) chart to show how the new major project will integrate actions for change, copies need to be circulated

A decision needs to be made on the style of communication to be used. What is the main message that the strategic integration group wants to communicate? What will be the best medium to do this? How will everyone be kept up to date with progress? All or any of the following methods might be considered:

- video
- company-wide briefing/conferences
- briefings to managers followed by line manager briefings to employees
- preparation of briefing packs
- regular newsletters
- articles in company magazines
- involving prestigious speakers in company briefings
- setting up a change project office.

Ownership, Involvement and Commitment

At this point, we must not forget the importance of OIC!

One of the main benefits of adopting a competence approach is the opportunity to involve the entire workforce in developments and thus to generate ownership and commitment.

It is therefore essential that, when considering communication issues, these three key aspects of the integrative approach are given priority consideration.

The Next Steps

As is no doubt obvious at this point, planning and building the framework are by no means minute tasks. Careful planning is however a keystone for success of any project – and it is lack of planning which itself leads to initiative overload.

Once the framework is in place, with clear lines of responsibility and communication, work on establishing a common language can begin, and it is not long after this that the benefits of the integrative approach begin to become apparent.

CASE STUDY: NETWORK SOUTHEAST

The following case study, kindly provided by Network SouthEast, a business sector of the British Railways Board, illustrates how the common language provided by a competence approach can begin to integrate initiatives and provide a common framework for individual and organizational development needs. This particular case study also illustrates four key issues which are dealt with in more detail in later chapters.

First, the study illustrates how a company can experience the value of a competence-based system (referred to as a standards-based framework), in a limited area of its operation, and then identify the potential for full integration within its overall approach to quality. Network SouthEast's initial experience with supervisory competences opened the door to integration and the establishment of a new overarching initiative to encompass a very wide range of organizational developments.

Second, an issue of particular interest is Network SouthEast's experience with (UK) nationally-derived (as opposed to company-derived) standards of performance. This is discussed in more depth in Chapter 8.

Third, is the issue of assessment of competence. The terminology used in this case study relates to the UK model of assessment for certification in the new National Vocational Qualification framework. The organization's experience with a competence-based approach raised questions concerning *who* assesses performance, *how* performance is assessed and how the *quality* of assessment is maintained.

Last, but by no means least, is the issue of *roles.* This is an important aspect of a competence-based approach, and one which provides enormous potential for organization development. Further guidance on this issue is given in the following chapter.

Network SouthEast

The Business

The South Central Division of Network SouthEast covers an area from London to Bexhill in East Sussex and Chichester in West Sussex and employs approximately 6,000 people. The revenue generated from the 373 route miles is around £158 m per annum. Over 1,600 trains run each work day through 178 stations. Network SouthEast is committed to ensuring that all staff at all levels have the opportunity to gain a UK National Vocational Qualification by 1999.

Background

Validation of the supervisory standards produced by the Management Charter Initiative (MCI) took place involving a number of supervisors and managers from differing backgrounds within Network SouthEast before a pilot programme commenced within the South Central Division. A former executive director at MCI (Management Charter Initiative, UK) was appointed by Network SouthEast as external advisor to assist in the implementation of standards-based development at Level 3 and above throughout the company.

Programme Outline

This programme, based on the MCI standards and leading to a BTEC/NVQ Level 3 qualification in Supervisory Management had the type of systematic approach that is needed for standards-based development:

1. Relating the national standards to the supervisor's own role.
2. Assessing current competences and development needs.
3. Introducing flexible development strategies based in the workplace.
4. Regular reviewing of performance by line managers.
5. Developing a portfolio of evidence by the supervisor.
6. Formal assessment of the evidence against national standards by an assessment panel.

A group of 40 supervisors from four functions (retail, fleet,

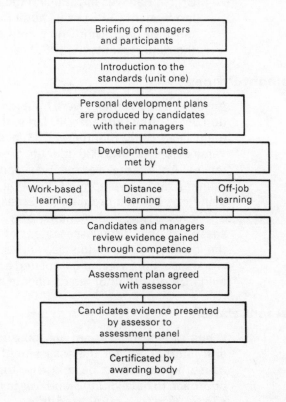

Figure 5.8 *Programme outline*

operations, infrastructure) started the pilot in November 1991. After completing Unit One of the Supervisory standards, candidates chose whether to take the remaining six units.

Unit One (Maintain Services and Operations to Meet Quality Standards) was completed first for the following reasons:

1. Quality, quantity, safety, delivery and cost specifications are the basis of performance measurements; this unit would ensure that they would be in place at any location involved in standards-based development.
2. The unit complemented British Rail's 'Quality through People' policy.
3. BS5750 was being introduced at many locations

throughout British Rail and Unit One would complement its introduction.

4. British Rail was introducing the International Safety Rating System (ISRS) as its audit process; personal competence through Unit One would assist managers to meet the requirements of ISRS.

The Assessment Process

Assessors and verifiers were trained from within the organization by Godfrey Durham (UK) Ltd to the Training and Development Lead Body Standards D33 (assess candidate using diverse evidence) and D36 (identify previously acquired competence). An internal verifier was appointed from within the training and development function, who undertook TDLB standards D34 (co-ordinate the assessment process).

The assessor, line manager and candidate agreed an assessment plan. After assessment of the portfolio, checks on the quality of the evidence, and direct assessment at the workplace, the assessor completed a report and presented the evidence on behalf of the candidate at an assessment panel.

The Assessment Panel

While direct verification was possible through an assessor and internal verifier the assessment panel was adopted because it was felt to be a crucial tool in ensuring a quality approach to developing standards in the workplace. The panel can be used for a number of different NVQs, but is particularly relevant at Level 3 and above where assessment is more complex than at the lower levels.

The panel is made up of a minimum of four assessors, internal verifier, external advisor and on occasions a moderator/external verifier from the awarding body. Assessors take it in turns to present candidate portfolios and then to sit on the main panel. It works through four stages:

- *Prior production of evidence*
- – The panel splits into small groups and checks individual pieces or tags of evidence for validity, currency, authenticity and sufficiency.
- *Presentation to the panel*
- – The assessor presents the assessment plan and method

of assessment to the panel. The assessor can also ask for guidance on any aspect of the evidence which may cause any doubt or uncertainty.

- *Questioning on the assessment process*
- Members of the panel will ask questions and give the assessor feedback on the assessment process.
- *Agreement*
- In most cases the panel will endorse the assessors' judgement; where it fails to do so differences can be noted for future guidance and consistency.

The assessment panel has been very successful in ensuring:

Objectivity	– judgements are made against the national standards and evidence requirements.
Credibility	– it is a very open process; the panel has high integrity within the organization.
Guidance	– assessment panels offer regular opportunities for assessors to receive guidance and feedback.
Consistency	– any problems of assessment or evidence requirements can be debated, resolved and corrective action implemented immediately, resulting in a consistent approach by all assessors.
Development	– the panel approach is an effective learning forum consistent with assessment of competence in the work place.
Flexibility	– the panel can be used for any approved standards-based programme and will be used for Management Level 1 and 2 and for assessor accreditation.
Quality	– the panel can meet the criteria listed above, respond to the changing needs of its customers (business, candidates and line managers) and meet national standards.

On 1 January 1992 the Division became the first business in the UK to gain approval from BTEC to offer a Continuing Education Certificate in Supervisory Management using the MCI Supervisory standards.

Its assessment process won particular praise from the BTEC moderator. After his first visit to an assessment panel he wrote in his report under Internal Monitoring of Assessment:

exemplary practice – the assessment panel carries out this function every 6–8 weeks undertaking a major quality control role. Procedures are extremely thorough.

Candidate Progress

The first two performance criteria in Unit One of the Supervisory standards caused problems for many supervisors. They are:

1.1 (a) Operations and services satisfy delivery, quantity and cost requirements.
1.1 (b) Work activities consistently meet quality, safety and delivery specifications.

Some of the functions involved had their own standards. This was to assist candidates who had quality measures and targets in place.

Candidates in other parts of the organization where standards were not in place were to face problems. It is obviously difficult to prove these performance criteria if output specifications and requirements are not fully stated. This also indicated a lack of clarity about role both for supervisor and manager.

Where candidates had difficulty proving competence as a result of a lack of quality specification, managers were questioned as they would need help to increase their own areas of competence. This led to two new initiatives:

1. The quality manager and the training and development manager were asked to provide consultancy support in order to put specifications in place formally or to develop clear delivery requirements.
2. It was now seen as essential that standards-based development should be implemented at all levels of management throughout the organization. It would also help managers understand more fully their role in developing their staff and the benefits of standards-based development both for them and the organization.

It proved the connection between quality and standards-based development for people at differing levels of the organization.

Links between the standards and other organizational issues began to surface and, less than one year after the pilot programme had started, Network SouthEast launched its 'Plan for People'.

A Plan for People

The key element of a Plan for People is for competence standards to provide a common framework for a wide variety of organizational and individual development needs, reflected by:

- quality, safety, finance and resource requirements;
- job descriptions, appraisal, selection, training;
- person specifications, succession planning;
- development initiatives, both personal and organizational.

As the quality initiative spreads throughout the organization a new dimension is being added to its development.

Conclusion

The principle of a standards-based framework encompassing personal and organizational initiatives provides us with a clear criteria for quality assurance measurement.

REVIEW

- Establish strategic management group
- Establish strategic integration group
- Agree workable mission statement, values, standards
- Clarify objectives
- Generate a sense of importance – communicate

6 The Operational Plan

> SUMMARY <

In this chapter:
- Issues such as ownership, involvement and commitment are reviewed.
- The importance of a common language is outlined together with suggestions for development.

ESTABLISH STARTING POINT
(the current organizational map)

CLARIFY OBJECTIVES
(the strategic management group)

ESTABLISH AN INTEGRATION FRAMEWORK
(the strategic integration group)

DEVISE OPERATIONAL PLAN
(a common language)

DEVELOP STAFF
(resourcing development and operation)

IMPLEMENT MONITOR AND EVALUATE
(expand integration)

Figure 6.1 *The Operational Plan*

Overview

Many competency-based projects focus on a narrow perspective, aiming to improve performance in one isolated area and never relating back to the business perspective. This results in standards being defined for one employee group only. Issues of how these standards will be assessed, or implications for other employee groups, for performance appraisal, recruitment systems, or for incentive systems, are not considered, yet they are all sure to come under scrutiny once competence-based standards are introduced, such is the effect of a competence-based system. For this reason, top-down commitment and a top-down approach are essential.

With a competence-based approach we can link *individual performance* directly to the *required business performance* – and *plan* an approach which improves many other aspects of business operation in an integrated project for continuous improvement. We can also cut costs by planning this integrated approach, thus avoiding the round of *ad hoc* project planning and investment. In addition, we can provide a common language which forms the basis for all future developments – but only if we start at the top and only by taking a long-term perspective.

Starting at the top means identifying mission and objectives – a process we examined in Chapter 5. In the approach outlined in this book, we are also integrating all other projects and initiatives, thus providing not only a common language for the achievement of business objectives, but also gaining the greatest value from all initiatives aimed at improving quality of product, service and people performance.

Starting at the Top

If we are aiming to improve quality, then we are aiming to encompass all aspects of business operation in that quality improvement, including culture, products, services and people.

To do so, we need a sense of direction and can establish this as discussed in Chapter 5. Our starting point must be what the company wants to achieve, and this must take into account planned change.

Plans for new plant, equipment, processes, employee levels – all must be considered at the outset and incorporated into our defined mission and company objectives by the strategic management group and strategic integration group at the planning stage. With the framework planned and the central management teams in place, work on defining a common language starts with the mission statement – which, for simplicity, we will refer to as the key purpose of the company.

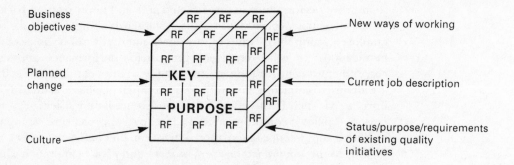

Figure 6.2 *Unpacking the key purpose*

Unpacking the Key Purpose of the Company

This activity needs to be undertaken by a project team which understands and applies the principles and the methods outlined in this chapter.

When adopting a competence-based approach, it is essential that the project team is able to differentiate between *what has to be achieved* and *who has to achieve it*. This is the basis on which unpacking of the key purpose is undertaken. A key purpose, when well-defined, should state what the company aims to achieve within the foreseeable future; it reflects the key areas of business activity and the perceived competitive advantage and/or consumer benefits.

The key purpose is made up of a number of role functions.

The term 'function' can be interpreted in several different ways. For some companies, a 'function' equates to a business unit; for others a 'function' is an operational centre. Most people think of 'functions' as representing a particular area of work and are concerned that 'functional analysis' results in something of a chimney stack approach to an organizational analysis – everything neatly compartmentalized in one 'chimney' or another. Yet further confusion is caused when a 'functional' map/chart/tree is related directly to an 'organizational' map/chart/tree, the latter illustrating who does what within the company. We need to clarify the interpretation of 'function' in this context.

Each role function represents one aspect of *what has to be achieved* within a company. The collective role functions correlate to the required business achievement. In this type of analysis, therefore, *who* achieves or *who* undertakes any activity is irrelevant. Similarly, a role function is not

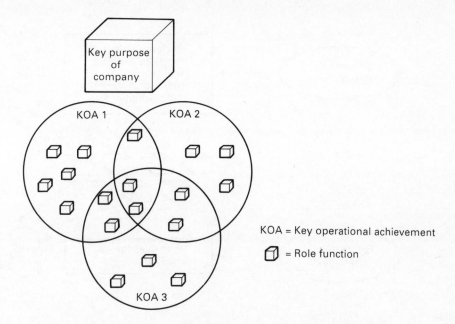

Figure 6.3 *Role functions as building blocks of company achievement*

simply activity undertaken within a particular business unit or operational centre – employees in different business units or different departments may undertake identical functions, but the combination of functions undertaken by each of these employees will vary.

This no doubt sounds even more confusing – so let's make it simpler to understand with some illustrations. Fig 6.2 illustrates how the role functions collectively meet the required achievements of the company. It also shows some of the other operational aspects of the business which must be taken into account when establishing what these role functions are.

The process of functional analysis must be undertaken *with* employees – not as an interview or questioning technique applied *to* them. Everyone in the company has valuable information; an experienced and client-centred analyst will use interviews, desk research and workshops to establish the analysis results, and to maintain the distinction between *what has to be achieved* and *who actually achieves it*. Remember our focus is on the former.

It is also important that perceived fears and threats of the new approach are dealt with at this time. Despite careful communication methods, there will still be concern about terms such as 'standards' or

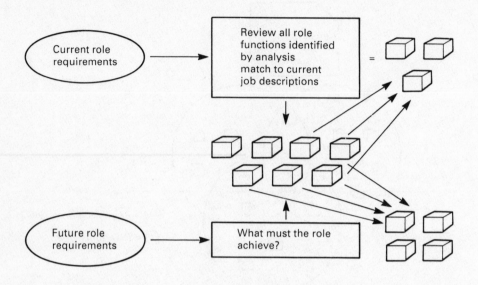

Figure 6.4 *Grouping role functions to define and structure roles*

'competences' or 'assessment'. One aspect of planned change is the reduction of staff levels – the company's approach to this will have been discussed by the strategic integration group .

The analysis itself is not a lengthy process. The company project team can be trained to undertake the main data collection (and to generate ownership, involvement and commitment); support from an experienced consultant need only be on a background support basis.

The analysis will review key operational achievements – and produce draft role functions. It is probably easiest to think of these in terms of building blocks of company achievement. Each building block represents something which has to happen and which contributes to achievement of the company objectives.

Each operational area of an organization will require that a number of role functions are achieved. Some of these role functions will also be relevant to other operational areas, as illustrated in Figures 6.3 and 6.4. By identifying the transferability of role function in this way, a valuable tool for employee mobility begins to emerge.

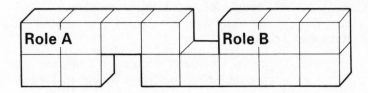

Figure 6.5 *Mobility of staff through role functions*

Role Functions and Job Descriptions

In one major corporation where this approach was applied, from the key purpose of the organization, 200 unit functions were identified. These were used as the basis for redefining and restructuring roles throughout the organization, providing flexibility and mobility of staff in the newly defined 35 roles. Prior to this, the organization had over 900 job descriptions, each relating to a particular area of work, but no way of identifying how to transfer relevant skills and knowledge from one area to another.

Another example is a large group which had over 2,000 job descriptions and was able to rationalise these to 14 key roles for its competence-based developments.

Role Functions and Role Mapping

The real value of identifying role functions in this way can perhaps be seen in Figures 6.3 and 6.4 which show how role functions can be grouped, or regrouped to meet operational needs.

The identified role functions, representing as they do a collective view of everything that needs to be achieved to achieve the company objectives, provide a basis on which role planning can be undertaken.

Role Functions and Mobility of Staff

Similarly, mobility of staff, transfer of skill and identification of dormant skills can be facilitated through reference to the same basis of role functions. Figure 6.5 illustrates how roles within a company may contain the same role function(s). Transfer from one role to another can therefore be managed by training and development in the role functions which are unique to the new role.

89

Dormant skills and knowledge can also be accessed both by the company and by the individual through identification of role functions related to the current or proposed area of work and assessment of relevant competence being undertaken.

Role Functions and Teams

The same principle of referring to a database of role functions can apply when establishing project or operational teams. The first decision is, 'What do we want the team to achieve?' Reference to the database of role functions will provide a combination of these 'building blocks' to define the team activities. Further reference to assessment records will indicate which individuals are competent in these role functions and thus the project or operational team can be created.

Developing Competences

Using the draft role functions, and the defined combinations of these role functions into the required roles, workshops with role holders can then be conducted to identify competences.

In the UK model, these competences will take the form of:

element + performance criteria + range statement

and will reflect the critical outcomes of workplace performance.

Other models may require that competences are identified in the form of:

dimensions → clusters → attributes

The key aspects of identifying competences should always relate to their assessment. There is little point in the roleholder defining competences if they cannot be assessed, or if their definition leaves interpretation open and thus affects the reliability of assessment.

Related to this is the need to express competences in language which will be understood by all users. Guidance on writing competence statements can be found in a variety of publications, some of which are listed in the reference section.

Integrating other Initiatives

In a TQM programme, we expect people to behave in a certain way, or to respond to customers in a certain way, or to operate in a quality team in a certain way. Similarly, with ISO9000 or BS5750, we expect certain activities to be undertaken in the workplace to ensure quality of our products and services. When writing competences for people we must ensure that these behaviours and activities are reflected in the competences we write.

The development activities should therefore be planned to incorporate these aspects of other quality initiatives. Results of competence development workshops should be discussed with project managers from the TQM, BS5750/ISO9000 and other projects to check whether the desired outcomes are being expressed in the standards of performance we are defining. Once again, the issue of assessment must be uppermost – will we be able to assess what we are defining? What evidence of competence will individuals and/or teams be able to produce to demonstrate their competence? How long is assessment likely to take?

The example in Figure 6.6 illustrates how this integration can take place. (See also p. 39 for previous example). This example has a customer focus and requires that individuals being assessed are constantly reviewing possibilities for improvement in business operations. It therefore sets the expectations of competent technical performance in the context of other quality initiatives such as customer care and continuous improvement. It also centres on both internal and external customers and the teamwork approach required in the working context. We could extend this still further with reference to BS5750/ISO9000 documentation in the range of records.

Consultation

To continue the development of ownership, involvement and commitment, the first draft competences should be circulated to all role holders for comment. Briefings with line managers are of great value in this respect so that line managers can themselves discuss the drafts with individuals and groups.

Consultation workshops may also be run, both with role holders and with their line managers. The results of this consultation must be collated and key issues identified and resolved.

When all this activity is complete, we will have standards of competence (or competences) for all role holders. If the development work has been extended across all roles within an organization, we will have standards of competence which reflect every role function and therefore every aspect of business performance.

Furthermore, the competences will have been developed *by and for* employees. Having been involved in their development, a sense of ownership will have been created and an understanding of their value already appreciated.

Unit 1

Activities

Provide technical advice	Assess technical requirements
	Provide analysis and recommendations

Activity 1.1 Assess technical requirements

Performance Criteria:

a   Assessment provides a solution which is fit for the purpose.
b   Customer's needs are correctly interpreted.
c   Nature and extent of problem is checked and confirmed.
d   Expert advice is sought when request for advice is outside the limits of individual expertise.
e   Options are fully explored with the customer.
f   Customer is fully supported and coached on the implementation of solutions.
g   Assessment takes account of site considerations, British standards and health and safety regulations.
h   Records are accurate and complete.

Range:

Recommendations on: Solutions to non-compliance of plant and equipment, suggestions for improvement to plant and equipment and development of personnel.

Customers: Project teams and managers, external customers and suppliers, finance, senior managers/directors, operators, training department.

Solutions: Long- and short-term, temporary.

Records: Manual, computerized and video.

Evidence:

Performance: Observation of assessments and solutions.
Effects of corrective action.
Customer reports on past assessments and solutions.
Written reports on past assessments and solutions.

Knowledge: Statutory health and safety and hygiene requirements relevant to location, equipment and type of assessment.
Industry standards, risk assessment, operational philosophy.
Interpersonal skills, technical skills.

Figure 6.6 *Example of integrative competence-based standard*

92

The involvement of employees and the consultation process undertaken will result in the production of a common language at two levels of the company.

1. Standards of performance (competences) for all employees, which can be used as the basis for:

   - training and development, design and delivery;
   - recruitment and selection;
   - performance appraisal;
   - continuous assessment;
   - professional development programmes.

2. A database of role functions which can be used as a basis for:

   - role structuring;
   - manpower planning;
   - project team planning;
   - career planning;
   - succession planning;
   - pay and incentive schemes (including certification and national recognition).

The Need for a Common Language

Perhaps the most difficult, but also the most exciting step for any organization is providing a common language. It is this aspect of the model which generally creates the highest level of interest in companies all around the world.

In any company review of its initiatives, we find that the TQM programme has its own terminology, so does the BS5750 quality procedures project, whilst the customer care programme has still other concepts and terms which need to be learned and applied. All of these initiatives affect what the company wants people to do and how well it wants them to do it. But if there is confusion about terms and initiatives, how can a harmonious and successful change programme be achieved? If the company is to be successful it needs to answer two major questions:

- What is the company aiming to achieve?
- What should each employee be doing to help achieve it?

Obvious questions, but rarely asked, never mind answered! And yet, the tools which provide the solution have been developing over the last two decades. The problem has been that these valuable tools have been developed and used for other purposes. My work in the last few years has been focused on modifying and extending these developments, to increase their potential use and thus their value to individual organizations.

The Untapped Potential of Competence as a Common Language

The 1990s has seen a great deal of activity at national level in respect of competence-based systems and competence-based standards. The main focus for this activity, in many parts of the world, has been on the review of qualifications systems. Industries and governments have worked on the definition of competence-based standards which can form the foundation for a new breed of qualifications.

These developments are revolutionary in that they provide individuals with recognition for what they can do rather than what they know. They allow individuals to achieve qualifications one stage at a time, simply by doing the work they would normally do. Other 'added value' aspects of this system include more involvement by managers in the day-to-day performance of company employees, as the operation of the qualification system centres on workplace assessment.

Despite these benefits, the new qualification systems are not achieving the success they should. Debates all over the world continue, with charges of 'over-bureaucratic systems', 'focus on the generic' and 'rigidity' becoming more and more common.

Having been involved in these developments at government and industry levels, I have some sympathy with these complaints. I have seen national developments begin with a flurry of excitement about industry involvement and a 'tool for business improvement'. However, as government budgets are cut and national coordinating bodies are established, this 'industry lead' diminishes; new criteria and requirements are introduced, the focus on the generic and transferable climbs to unusable proportions and flexibility fades.

This is a great pity, as the competence-based system can be of tremendous value to individual organizations, if it is developed and used to its full potential – and from the right starting point. My work over the last two years has indicated that a competence-based system can provide the foundation for integrating quality; it can provide the common language and thus the basis for efficient and cost-effective planning and review of all human resource activities, from recruitment and selection through career structures to pay and incentive systems and manpower planning.

Most recent work has shown that using the full potential of a competence-based system, and combining this with software applications, extends the use of the model still further as a powerful planning and organization development tool.

Creating the Common Language

To establish the common language, the standards of performance for each identified role function must be developed by employees themselves – thus creating ownership, involvement and commitment. Because we want this common language to incorporate all aspects of other quality initiatives, we must plan these developments to ensure that this occurs.

Figures 6.7, 6.8 and 6.9 illustrate how this happens with respect to BS5750, ISO9000 and TQM.

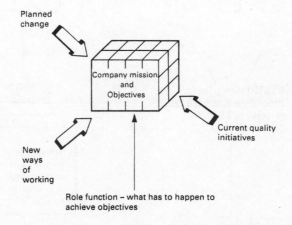

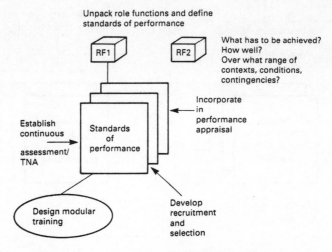

Figure 6.7 *Competence and BS5750/ISO9000/TQM*

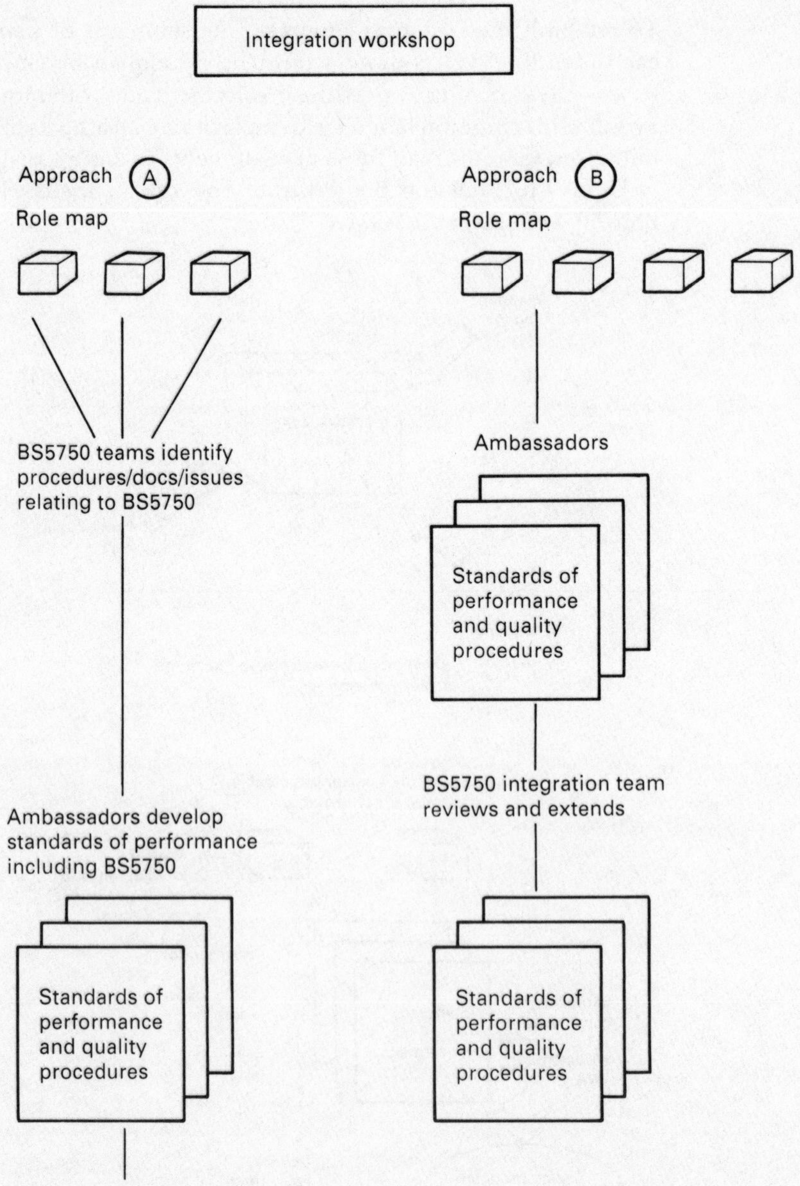

Integration workshop

Approach (A)

Role map

Approach (B)

Role map

BS5750 teams identify
procedures/docs/issues
relating to BS5750

Ambassadors

Standards of
performance
and quality
procedures

Ambassadors develop
standards of performance
including BS5750

BS5750 integration team
reviews and extends

Standards of
performance
and quality
procedures

Standards of
performance
and quality
procedures

Figure 6.8 *Competence and BS5750/ISO9000 – integrating through standards*

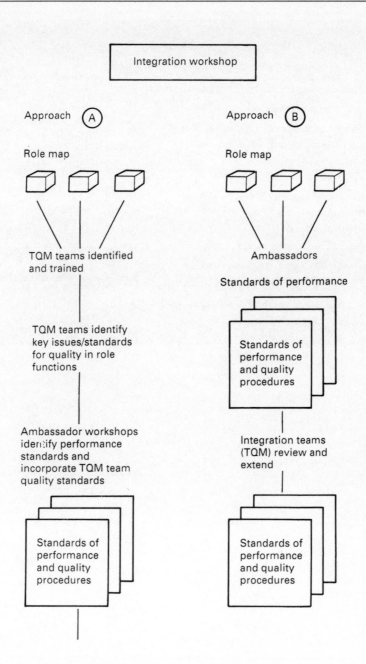

Figure 6.9 *Competence and TQM – integrating through standards*

REVIEW

The operational plan should allow for the following:

1. Role/remit of strategic management group
2. Role/remit of strategic integration group
3. Expertise and resources to undertake
   - Function mapping
   - standards definition
   - consultation on standards.
4. Expertise and resources to undertake
   - Role mapping
   - consultation.
5. Further planning to undertake extension of use of the mapping exercise and the common language which results (see Chapter 7).
6. Plans for ensuring integration with other quality initiatives (see Figures 6.6 – 6.9).
7. Expected outcomes/deliverables.
8. Timescale for developments.

7 Implementing the System

▷   SUMMARY   ◁

This chapter:
* explores issues of implementation and staff development:
  – the development phase;
  – the implementation phase.

ESTABLISH STARTING POINT
(the current organizational map)

CLARIFY OBJECTIVES
(the strategic management group)

ESTABLISH AN INTEGRATION FRAMEWORK
(the strategic integration group)

DEVISE OPERATIONAL PLAN
(a common language)

DEVELOP STAFF
(resourcing development and operation)

IMPLEMENT, MONITOR AND EVALUATE
(expand integration)

Figure 7.1 *Implementing the system*

Development Phase

This phase relates to all aspects of design and development of the integrated quality and competence system. Those who undertake these developments will need to be competent in the following areas:

- Methodology of functional analysis and its application at organizational level.
- Methodology of competence-based standards development and its application at organizational level.
- Concepts and operation of other quality initiatives such as BS5750/ISO9000, TQM, etc (as relevant to your organization's context).
- Design of supporting in-house assessment and quality assurance system.
- Negotiations with awarding bodies of your choice if national recognition is one objective of your development phase.

Getting Help

Guidance on a national perspective to functional analysis is available in a number of publications including those produced by the UK Department of Employment (Training Agency, 1989–91). Other publications by national bodies involved in the development of new competence-based qualification systems provide further guidance and case studies.

It may be that external help is required for this aspect of developments. When selecting external support, it is essential that you clearly define the organization's needs for an integrated approach, not simply a nationally focused methodology. Ask external providers to show you examples of previous work, and obtain references from previous clients.

Also explore, in depth, how external support can help you to develop your own staff to undertake the main part of the work (assuming you can allocate the resources). This will provide a more cost effective approach.

Implementation Phase

This relates to the introduction of the system, once developed. You will require the following staff skills:

- competence-based assessment;
- quality assurance/verification;
- training design using competence-based standards;

- training delivery using competence-based standards;
- performance appraisal design.

You may find that the skills required go beyond this list. This is because of the ripple effect that the use of a common language on a competence basis can have.

The Ripple Effect

Figure 7.2 illustrates how competence-based standards – those which incorporate the requirements not only of technical and personal competence, but also those of effective operation within other quality initiatives – can form a nucleus for change across a broad spectrum of human resource activities. The use of such a standards-based system (as illustrated in the Network SouthEast Case Study) stimulates such change.

For example, in one company, standards of this kind were developed firstly on the basis of a need to improve the design and delivery of technical training. However, once the system became operational, the managers involved asked for development in questioning and feedback skills; then in coaching and on-job development skills. Trainers were also trained in the use of the standards as a basis for training design.

The personnel department then reviewed and redesigned the performance appraisal system using the common language of organizational standards; career structure was reviewed using the role mapping output and incentive schemes were planned on the basis of reward for competence (quality) performance.

The system of recording assessment and training needs provided the documentation required for the BS5750 system. Networking of assessors and team briefings also provided the forum for total quality teams.

Thus the ripple effect operates. The remainder of this chapter provides guidance to help you with planning both the implementation and the staff development needs required for that implementation. Several ripples are addressed. These are:

- Competence and assessment
- Competence and quality managers
- Competence and time management
- Competence and quality training
- Competence and quality selection and recruitment
- Competence and performance appraisal
- Competence and quality incentive systems

This book can only provide a brief overview of each of these areas. However, I hope that the following text provides a sufficient guide to get

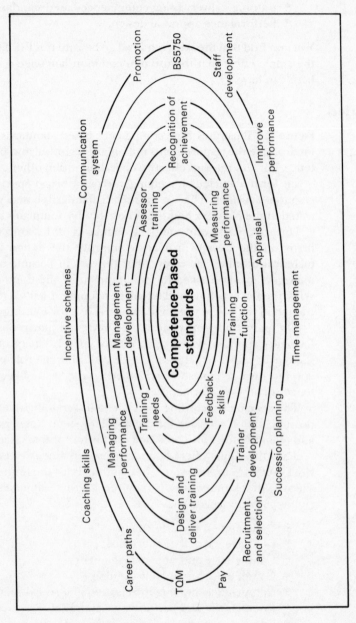

Figure 7.2 *The ripple effect*

you started and ensure that you consider all possible angles of the ripple effect in your own context.

Competence and Assessment

The introduction of a competence-based system requires a quality assessment mechanism. There is little point in having standards (competences) which reflect the required performance of individuals and teams if they are expressed in terms which no one can understand, or if the cost of assessing them is prohibitive.

Readers might wish to refer to my earlier book, *Competence-Based Assessment Techniques* for a detailed approach to competence-based assessment. For the purpose of this book, I propose to outline the key issues which will influence decisions regarding the design of an appropriate assessment mechanism.

Perhaps one of the very first questions to be asked when considering the introduction of competences is, 'Who will do the assessment?' To answer this, we first have to be clear that competence-based assessment is continuous assessment. Whilst competences can be used as the foundation for the design of a performance appraisal system along the more traditional (annual) assessment of performance route, competence-based systems are designed for more regular performance measurement.

The best place to measure performance on a regular basis is in the workplace, which means that the best people to undertake assessment are line managers who are monitoring and measuring performance of their employees on a day-to-day basis. (This is not always possible for operational reasons, although one might question why a line manager would be responsible for someone he or she rarely has contact with.) However, where line managers are unable to undertake full responsibility for assessment, a system of multiple assessors can be introduced, perhaps with the candidate taking a key role in their own assessment process through the collation of quality evidence of performance.

The issue of evidence is the second most important factor to consider. Assessment of competence (in respect of competent workplace performance) requires that evidence of performance is generated, collected and judged.

It is a misconception that assessors need checklists for each and every 'element' of a standards-based system. Encouraging assessors to use checklists does little to improve the quality of assessment. Assessors who follow assessment guidelines which state, for example, 'observe performance in this element on three occasions' are being encouraged to com-

103

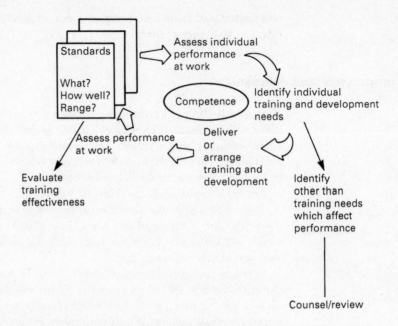

Figure 7.3 *Competence and continuous assessment*

plete a ticklist which merely indicates 'how many' and not 'how well'. I can easily complete a checklist which states that I have observed performance on the required number of occasions; this would say little about the quality of the performance I observed.

A quality assessment system has quality assessors – those who understand and can apply basic principles of competence-based assessment; who recognize quality evidence and who can encourage and support individuals to produce the high quality evidence required. They will also be able to identify training needs. All this suggests that the quality of assessor training is paramount to the success of the assessment mechanism.

Similarly, an assessment system will only be successful if it is user-friendly. Piles of checklists, evidence records and achievement forms will do little to help morale or improve quality. In designing an assessment system, ease of use should be a priority. This means taking into account the operational context.

When considering assessment issues, therefore, the following should be kept in mind:

- Who will assess – single or multiple assessors?
- Is it user-friendly – does it meet operational needs?

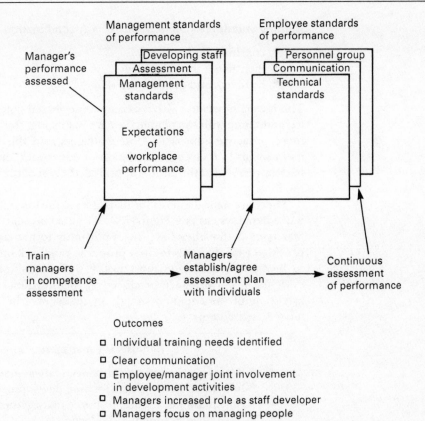

Outcomes

☐ Individual training needs identified

☐ Clear communication

☐ Employee/manager joint involvement
in development activities

☐ Managers increased role as staff developer

☐ Managers focus on managing people

Figure 7.4 *Competence and management development*

- Is assessor training encouraging the development of assessors who both understand and apply principles?
- Will it meet criteria for planned external agency involvement?

The last point concerns plans for national certification. A company may wish to provide certification as one of the ripple effects of the introduction of a competence-based system.

Competence and Quality Managers

If managers are to be assessors, there are obvious implications for them both as individuals and as managers.

When competence-based systems are introduced into a company, one of the first requests from line managers in their assessor role is for training and development in one or any combination of the following:

- coaching skills
- identifying training needs
- feedback and questioning skills

This is usually because within a competence-based system, managers have to spend time with the people they are managing; they have to develop a more proactive approach. Most managers find this difficult. Management seems to focus on completion of paperwork; employees get feedback once a year at the annual appraisal; the rest of the year managers are too busy.

There are many benefits for managers in the introduction of a competence-based system (see Figure 7.4). We could say that a major benefit for managers is that they have an opportunity to manage – and they are provided with the tools to do it properly. Feedback on performance has to be fair, as managers must justify their decisions by reference to evidence of performance produced by the individual and team. Fig 7.5 lists some of the comments made by managers who are using competence-based systems.

Benefits for managers

- Business-oriented performance management.
- Individual and business-focused development.
- Consistency of human resource management.
- Guides recruitment and selection.
- Everyday practical mechanism for managing more effectively.
- Objective succession planning.
- Common language/clear communication.

Figure 7.5 *Benefits for managers*

Competence and Time Management

One key concern of managers at the early stages of competence development is time. This is partly because assessment is initially still seen as something independent of managing – something which is normally done by trainers or college lecturers and involves marking papers. Later, as the system is understood a little more clearly, the fears relate to having to spend time observing people work or talking to them and providing feedback.

Other objections may relate to the fact that managers have never been trained in a) managing people and b) managing their time. They may all have been issued with very elaborate time manager filofaxes, and have attended a short course – but how applicable is all this to what they actually do? How many managers actually use their time management system? How many use it effectively?

Introducing a competence based system raises lots of questions, some about the current performance of managers and all other groups of employees; but just as many about the company operation – its generation of paperwork, its expectation of managers, its support through training and development, its review of role structures, career structures, and its use of dormant skills.

Competence and Quality Training

Once competence-based standards and assessment are introduced and assessment is undertaken on a continuous basis, training needs will be identified. Hopefully, managers will have been supported by training and development in the identification of training needs (not *all* poor performance is due to a training need).

One of the first requirements to emerge will be the need for a clear communication channel along which training needs can be directed to a central source. The next requirement is that the central source can do something about the identified training needs! The opportunity to design training on a modular basis, targeted to individual and group training needs provides a huge potential for cost-saving on training and development. However, to be effective, those who design these training modules must understand the principles of competence-based standards and be able to design effective training which will develop competence to the required standards.

Training programmes can also provide opportunities for assessment and therefore generate supporting evidence of competence performance – another motivator for individuals to attend training.

The drive for training will also come from individuals themselves. Everyone can now take responsibility for their own development; everyone knows what standards are expected of them and how their combination of role functions relates to other people's roles. Motivation (and hopefully incentives) for progression vertically and laterally will be increased and, with it, the demand for training. Figure 7.6 illustrates how a modular approach to training and development can be adapted and provide real flexibility.

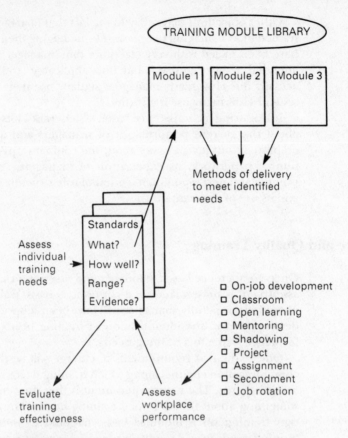

Figure 7.6 *Competence and training and development*

Competence and Quality Selection and Recruitment

Once again, the common language provided by competences and role functions can provide the foundation for recruitment and selection. New and existing roles can be defined by the combination of role functions required.

If internal assessment records are computerized, a search of the database will reveal employees who have demonstrated competence in the required role functions and transfer is therefore facilitated. For external recruitment, the common language provides the basis for the design of specifications and advertisements as well as the foundation for interview schedules.

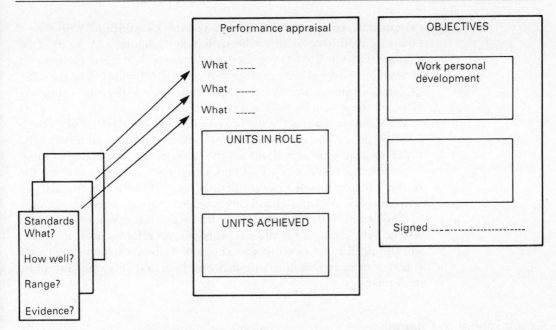

Figure 7.7 *Competence and performance appraisal*

Competence and Performance Appraisal

In performance appraisal, the common language of integrated competence/quality standards provides a basis on which annual reviews are related directly to on-going records of performance, not simply to what is often a subjective report. The key activities (or elements) of the standards used can be transposed to an appraisal document. Developmental plans will include further training and development to help individuals acquire the units relating to their current role, and to their career development plan. These plans can include activities such as projects which will provide the relevant opportunity for individuals to demonstrate competence.

Figure 7.7 illustrates the use of competence-based standards in an annual performance appraisal system.

Competence and Quality Incentive Systems

Perhaps one of the thorniest issues is pay and incentives. If a competence-based system is operational, what happens when individuals successfully demonstrate competence? Will they receive a certificate? Will it be a company certificate or will it be nationally recognized by an external agency? Will it link to a recognized qualification? Will it line them up for promotion? Will it give them more money? In short, what will be the value of demonstrating competence to the individuals within the company? How will the system be used as a motivational tool?

For some companies, the use of a competence-based system aligns with a review of pay and incentive schemes which is already underway. The RoleFunction approach allows for role structuring and facilitates more innovative approaches to pay systems. Length of service becomes less the norm, and pay linked to performance, together with incremental systems, succession planning and career progression are possible.

This is not to suggest that the introduction of a competence-based system is the panacea for all such problems. An effective and fair system will still need to be developed: a competence-based system simply provides a tool and a common language on which that development can be undertaken.

Commitment to Change

It may well be apparent from this short chapter that the introduction of a competence-based system can have far-reaching effects for a single company.

The potential value of the common language as an organizational development tool is enormous – and for this reason requires a top-down commitment to change.

Any organization considering the introduction of a competence-based system needs to be aware of the impact that this can have. Selling the benefits is easy once an organization has recognized the potential and/or experienced the use of such a system through an initial pilot. However, I would advise any client to consider and to plan for the implications involved – it may be a five-year plan, this doesn't all happen overnight, but a plan for change is essential, whatever the original driving force for the interest in competence.

REVIEW

The introduction of an integrated competence/quality standards-based system can have enormous impact on all human resource activities across the organization. When preparing your plan, therefore, you should consider how the introduction of this system will impact on:

- current methods of assessing performance;
- current performance appraisal systems;
- current selection and recruitment activities;
- current management development;
- current training and development;
- current incentive and reward systems;
- current career and progression routes;
- current multiskilling plans.

In addition, you need to take into account:

- planned change.

8 National and Organizational Perspectives

                                    SUMMARY

This chapter:
- will assist those organizations in countries where national development of competence-based qualifications systems is taking place.

A major consideration for companies in this situation is whether to adopt the nationally developed benchmark, or whether to establish their own standards of performance. This chapter outlines some of the key issues and implications involved. A decision can only be made when all relevant data have been collected and carefully considered in the light of business objectives. The following aims to help companies to make an informed decision.

National competence-based systems have much to recommend them. They provide a revolutionary approach to individual recognition and to the structuring and access arrangements for national qualifications.

Similarly, company-specific systems have particular benefits, which include competences linked directly to business performance, and an assessment system which meets operational needs as well as operating across all work roles. In addition, the use of role functions which have been identified from the company's own mission and objectives provide a valuable organizational development tool.

In practice, companies may make use of both nationally derived and company-specific systems. This chapter aims to help you to make an informed decision on how to adopt the best approach for your own organization.

Nationally Derived Competence-Based Systems

The development of national standards for certification purposes has been undertaken by the UK, Australia and New Zealand in recent years. Other countries are following suit.

The particular benefits of these systems include the provision of a common benchmark of performance with standards of performance agreed across an industry or a sector of industry. The standards are incorporated into 'units of competence' (UK) or 'units of learning' (NZ). In addition, the USA-derived competence-based systems utilize 'dimensions and clusters' in a model for the development of competence.

The 'units' or 'clusters' are grouped to form national qualifications. In the UK, a defined combination of units forms a National Vocational Qualification at one of five levels. In other systems, units can be cross-referenced to various degree programmes and provide credit towards a recognized qualification.

All operate on a credit accumulation system, providing access to nationally recognized awards on a 'one chunk at a time' basis.

Such systems are supported by individualized workplace assessment. Assessment requires that individuals provide evidence of competence which can be matched to the standards. This evidence is produced through normal workplace activity. Assessors must be trained and themselves demonstrate competence in their assessment role.

Difficulties with such systems arise for a number of reasons. Some find the standards too generic, with language which does not apply to their particular context or is not easily understood by users. Others find that the combination of units does not fit their needs, meaning that employees will never be able to achieve a full qualification. For others, the issue of assessment is the key difficulty. Within the UK qualification system for instance, national awarding bodies are the gatekeepers of the assessment process. When the standards are developed, assessment guidance and quality assurance procedures are agreed with the national industry body which has responsibility for the development of the competence-based qualification. Assessment documentation is then designed to enable records of evidence to be kept and notification of achievement to be forwarded to the awarding body.

For single qualifications this may not be a problem. But as the qualifications are designed for different occupational areas, and at different levels, a large organization may find it needs to introduce large numbers of qualifications for its employees. This requires that it introduces the assessment system designed for each specific qualification and this can

113

result in several different systems operating within one company, or even on one site. The cost of assessment then rises. Each qualification requires a registration fee for each assessment centre (ie, workplace); assessors must also be registered. Costs of external verification must be met as well as individual certification fees.

Governments provide incentives for these schemes. In the UK, the Investors in People Award, provided to organizations which meet specific standards, has a particular focus on the use of National Vocational Qualifications (NVQs). Employers are also entitled to claim a 25 per cent tax rebate on all NVQ-related training.

The difficulty is, however, that the benefits of the rebate have to be weighed against the costs of implementation for a real cost-saving to be calculated – and the calculation does not always come out on the side of implementation, especially when other issues of applicability and user-friendliness are taken into account.

It is, of course, possible to implement the national standards and to enhance these to meet organizational requirements. Some companies have done this and to great effect; others find that the effort required to do this is better spent on developing their own competences and assessment system in the first place.

Company-specific Systems

Opting for developing a purely company-specific scheme will depend upon the company commitment to change, and its perception of the real benefits to be gained from a competence-based approach.

If, as with many companies, the organization begins by acknowledging a need to review its training function, or its pay and incentive scheme, or perhaps its performance appraisal system, and sees a competence approach as valuable in this respect, it isn't too long before other benefits of the system become apparent. New developments then begin, which may include the definition of company-specific competences across the board.

The main benefit of a company-specific system is perhaps the ability to tailor the entire system to both current and future needs whilst developing a real sense of ownership. The implication, of course, is the need for long-term planning and to recognize the broader impact that competences can have on business operational structure and all human resource activity.

When it comes to the crunch, the decision to go for national or company specific systems will depend on the recognition of need for and overall commitment to change, and to continuous improvement in terms of company specific objectives. I would recommend that any company undertake careful planning and review of short- and long-term costs of both options before making a decision.

References and Further Reading

Campbell and Young (1990) *Do You Need a Mission Statement?*, Economist Publications.

Egan, G (1988) *Change Agent Skills*, CA: San Diego University Associates.

Fletcher, S (1991a) *NVQs Standards and Competence; A Practical Guide for Managers and Trainers*, London: Kogan Page in association with Godfrey Durham.

Fletcher, S (1991b) *Designing Competence-Based Training*, London: Kogan Page.

Fletcher, S (1992) *Competence-Based Assessment Techniques*, London: Kogan Page.

Hastings, C, Bixby, P and Chaudhry-Lawton, R (1986) *Superteams*, London: Fontana/Collins, Ashridge Management College.

National Center for Research in Vocational Education (1983) *Occupational Adaptability and Transferable Skills*, NCRVE, Ohio State University.

Oakland, J S (1989) *Total Quality Management*, Oxford: Butterworth-Heinemann.

Training Agency (1989–91) *The Development of Assessable Standards for National Certification*, Technical Advisory Group notes nos 1–6, Sheffield: Employment Department.

Weick, K E (1969) *The Social Psychology of Organizing*, Reading, MA: Addison Wesley.

Index

assessment
    of competence 101, 103
    competence-based 103
    continuous 104
    networking of assessors 101

BS5750
    accreditation 66
    audit 36, 41
    and competence 33, 41, 68, 95
    corrective action 36
    individual role within 29
    programmes 24
    quality assurance system 34
    quality manual 36
    work instructions 35

coaching skills 106
competence
    achievement-led system 20
    and assessment 103, 104
    -based assessment 103
    -based standards 39, 71, 93, 94, 98
    and BS5750 33 41, 67, 71, 90, 95
    as a common language 94
    developing 90
    development-led system 20
    and incentive systems 101, 110
    and performance appraisal 101, 109
    and quality divide 18, 41, 71
    and quality managers 101, 105
    and quality procedures 35, 41

    and selection and recruitment 101, 108
    and time management 101, 106
    and TQM 37, 41, 67, 71, 90, 97
    and training 101, 107
common language
    creating 95
    need for 71, 93
    potential of 94
commitment
    to all initiatives 76
    to change 110
    and ownership 76, 91
    top down 64, 76, 85
consultation
    on development of competences 91
    workshop 91
continuous improvement
    based development programmes 24
    definition 19
    process 41
costs of not integrating 20

developing staff
    competence needed 100
    development phase 100
downsizing
    requirement of restructuring 29

employee involvement
    in function mapping 87
    in all initiatives 38, 74, 76
    in TQM 37

framework
    building 74
    for integration 54, 61, 63
functions
    definition 86
    in roles 86
functional analysis
    process 87

getting help
    development phase 100
    implementation phase 100

IBIS model 24
implementing the system
    implementation phase 100
    planning implementation 99
incentive systems and competence 101, 110
initiative overload syndrome 46, 48, 49
integration
    competence and quality procedures 36, 38
    of planning and action 43, 44
    of quality and competence 20, 21, 42, 75, 90
integrative approach
    illustration of 68
    need for 22, 42
    process 90
ISO9000
    accreditation 66
    and competence 33, 42, 95

job descriptions and roles 89

key operational achievements
    definition 88
key purpose of company 67, 86

management development and competence 101,
        105
mapping
    matrix 53
    organization projects 52, 55, 70, 75
measuring performance
    benefits of 71
mission
    defining 67, 68

example mission statements 70
    statements 57, 65, 85
mobility of staff and role functions 89

objectives
    clarifying 66
    company 64–5
operational plan
    developing 84
ownership of initiatives 76

people gap
    acknowledging 71
performance appraisal
    integrating 38, 101, 109
planning
    and action dialogue 38, 43
    change 41, 76

quality
    assessment system 103
    assurance 19, 34, 100
    circles 37, 38
    definition 19
    initiatives 18, 33
    mission 57
    planning, gap in 66–7
    policy 56
    strategy 56
    values 57, 65
    vision 57

research
    company projects/initiatives 56
restructuring
    plans for 29
ripple effect
    definition and importance 101
role analyser 29
role function
    definition 86
    grouping 88
    and job description 89
    and mobility of staff 89–90
    and role mapping 89, 107, 112
    and teams 90

role mapping
    maps 24
    process 24
    and role functions 89
route map for company development 68

selection and recruitment and competence 101,
        108
standards
    company 65, 85, 112, 114
    national 85, 112, 113
    of performance 69
starting point for integration 47
strategy
    strategic intent 57
    strategic orchestra 57, 58
    strategic planning 57
    strategic thinking 66
    strategy formulation 57
strategy integration group
    role 68–9
    tasks 68–9

strategic management group
    role 64, 67
    tasks 64
survey task 1, initiatives 50

teams
    role 41
    and role functions 90
time management and competence 101, 106
tòtal quality
    and competence 19, 37, 42, 66, 97
    focus on 66
    individual role within 29
    programmes 19, 24, 37, 41, 42
training
    and competence 101, 107
    training needs 105

values
    clarifying 66
    company 64

work instructions 36